Obscurity and a competence – that is the life that is best worth living.

Mark Twain

One must choose between obscurity with efficiency, and fame with its inevitable collateral of bluff.

William McFee.

MEET THE RESIDENTS
AMERICA'S MOST ECCENTRIC BAND!

by
Ian Shirley

First published in 1993 by SAF Publishing Ltd.

SAF Publishing Ltd.
12 Conway Gardens,
Wembley, Middx.
HA9 8TR
ENGLAND
TEL: 081 904 6263

Cover photo: Poreknowgraphix

ISBN 0 946719 12 8

Printed in England by Redwood Books, Trowbridge, Wiltshire.

For Jenny, my wife, who after an intensive nine-month period still thinks The Residents are crap, and Thomasina my daughter who will grow up to know better.

ACKNOWLEDGEMENTS

Special thanks to Homer Flynn and Hardy Fox of the Cryptic Corporation for time, telephone numbers, hospitality and assistance in getting interviews and photographs together.

Special thanks also to Brian Poole and Edwin Pouncey for access to their archive material.

I would also like to thank the following people who graciously agreed to be interviewed in the preparation of this book (in alphabetical order): Laurie Amat, J. Raul Brody, Chris Cutler, Dianne Flynn, Andy Gill, John Kennedy, Carol LeMaitre, Sarah McLennan, Chris McGregor, Philip Perkins, Brian Poole, Edwin Pouncey, Rex Ray, Jon Savage, Rich Shupe, Tom Timony.

Thanks also to: Leigh Barbier, Harry Borden, Sheenah Fair, Jay Clem, Trev Faul, Mick Fish (editing), Simon Gregg, Dave Hallbery (design and layout), Val Harden, Matt Howarth, Penn Jillette, Randolph II (the Cryptic leather-eared cat), These Records and Peter Zumsteg.

CONTENTS

AUTHOR'S NOTE

The Residents have seen a draft of this book, having sent a copy to their management The Cryptic Corporation. They corrected some inaccuracies in the text, although in their opinion, "much of the writing is supposition rather than truth". They refer to some of my conclusions as "those weird Ian-isms", stating that they have never given interviews despite the evidence I possess and have quoted which suggests the contrary.

As the author of this book I would like to state that in researching and compiling my subject I have endeavoured to present as truthful and factual a history of The Residents as possible. In their final correspondence to me, The Residents themselves cautioned me by adding, "you must know that everyone you spoke with intentionally lied to you at some point." So, due to the web of myth, secrecy and downright occlusion of the truth that has always been part of their long and continuing career, I have to confess that in some instances I have had to use facts of dubious origin and hazard guesses at the truth.

This is their story, but my interpretation.

Who the hell are The Residents...1?
Cartoon by Savage Pencil from Rock and Roll Zoo

INTRODUCING THE RESIDENTS

"The music they played was a natural happiness of love, so rare I cannot explain it. It was fresh and courageous; daring, sincere, unfettered. It was unmanufactured avant-garde, and still is, because there was no place for it on the world; so the world neglected something of value and did not understand. And all along I could not understand why the world could not understand. It was all there. Was it because the world considers music as only a commercial commodity? I am glad that that is not my code."[1]

This is not someone talking about The Residents, but the unique Sun Ra talking about the great black territory bands that inspired him during his youth.

However in the same sort of way, The Residents inspired me during my youth. The 'Big Bang' that was punk rock created a whole new musical universe. Of course, although they rode to notoriety on the crest of this New Wave, The Residents were not of it. They had already been operating for some five years before the English music press stumbled across them in late 1977. Their music and whole concept was strikingly at odds with everything else on the market. I still vividly recall my first encounter with their totally original music. I bought the compilation album *Nibbles* after reading Edwin Pouncey's graphic review in *Sounds*. Typically I had a friend in tow and we went back to his place to listen to it, as well as his copy of Tubeway Army's *Replicas*. I can well remember his absolute look of pained incomprehension when tracks like "Constantinople", "Santa Dog '78" and "Semolina" bled their way out of his speakers. And that was just side one. We never got to side two. He took the record off, placed it in the sleeve as if were infected and turned to me and said for the tenth time in fifteen minutes, "You don't really like this do you? It's not music!"

Of course I was rather shell-shocked myself. This was a bit different from my regular musical diet of the time; typically Sex Pistols, The Clash, the original Ultravox, Cabaret Voltaire, Kraftwerk, Joy Division, Wire and Throbbing Gristle (a different type of noise), and yes, even for a brief time Gary Numan's Tubeway Army. However, for some reason I defended this latest purchase to my friend, and promptly stomped off to play it at home on my father's superior system. "What's this?" he said wafting into the room one night when I was playing *Meet The Residents*. "It sounds almost classical. Don't tell me you're acquiring musical taste buds at last?" I sneered at the time with the typical "what do you know about music" adolescent response, but he was a man who knew a classical and operatic motif when he heard one.

I grew to love The Residents. More importantly they threw my interest in music off into different musical tangents. They were sublimely educational. Their music did not just feed from the rock pool but embraced all manner of other types of musical influence, from contemporary classical, free jazz, big band swing, Eastern and African music as well as sugar pop. Ironically, this is why – image aside – they stirred so much interest when they broke upon these and other shores. Their music was a melange of styles that the limited rock listener simply did not know existed. These listeners may never have heard the names Stan Kenton, Perez "Mambo

King" Prado, Henry Mancini and Sun Ra – let alone appreciate their expressive horn arrangements. But The Residents did, and by cunning multi-tracking, incorporated them into one of many of their musical trademarks. To the rock fan, opera was a dirty word, but to The Residents it was a fluid form to tell musical stories. As for The Beatles and The Stones, they were considered passé, but The Residents took their music (and that of other sixties acts) behind their eight-track bicycle shed and gave it a loving sonic fuck.

They also used technology. Their sound always changing, shifting and metamorphasising with their influences, increasingly grasping musical form and mastery of recording techniques. They became obsessively interested in new developments. It was no accident that as their career developed, they pioneered the innovative use of synthesisers, original sampling technology and MIDI computerisation. However, they always used the technology to realise musical visions rather than simply for the sake of it.

Of course there has always been more to The Residents than the music. There is a whole mystery that surrounds their identities. They recognised at an early stage that it was not only music that sold records and fuelled interest, but the whole paraphernalia that surrounded the concept of a rock group. The packaging and promotion of records, image, attitude, personal habits – and most important of all – the whole mythology of how the musicians were perceived by their fans. The fetishistic nature that turns throwaway adolescent gestures into heroic acts. The type of mythology that transformed Paul McCartney's walking across a pedestrian crossing in Abbey Road barefoot into rumours that he was dead.

The Residents took all this to its logical extreme. They became visibly invisible. They refused to give interviews and submerged their egos beneath a faceless collectivism that defined The Residents as a "band" that refused to reveal their true identities like comic book super heroes. Of course, they were canny enough to release carefully staged publicity photographs which pictured the group in a variety of arresting disguises ranging from neo Ku Klux Klan newspaper outfits, to posing in a supermarket in radiation suits, before settling for their instantly recognisable eyeball and tuxedo combination.

This book is an attempt to correct an injustice. Despite ongoing projects of startling creativity, The Residents have been cruelly overlooked in recent years. Marginalised as obscurist practical jokers who are no longer funny. The Residents don't deserve to be dismissed that easily. Over twenty years of trading they have steadfastly refused to be anything other than themselves. They have never played it safe, constantly striving to put their creativity on the line, even if it meant alienating the very fans who sustained them.

Whatever critics thought, The Residents remained true to themselves. They have always perceived their music as a series of "experiments" rather than a string of contractual record releases. Some have been fantastically successful, whilst others have hit the wall at high speed. Like the late Sun Ra, they view each release less as an artefact than as a musical photograph taken at a particular stage in their ongoing explorations. The fact that these photographs might take years to develop is of no consequence to them. The fact that they have found a market for their product is only of interest to them because it allows them to continue, always owning, releasing or licensing their own product and exercising an iron control over what is made available. Like Frank Zappa, they strongly believe that only they have the right to document their career, even if that involves tweaking old recordings and destroying master tapes to ensure that no one will be able to second guess them when they are gone.

Ultimately, the cult of anonymity and attendant marketing scams have probably been too much for some. Inevitably, at one time or another, the question of The Residents' true identities, and how many of them there actually are, has received more attention than their music. A blatant exposé was never my purpose in writing a book about them and might in some ways disappoint those who expected to see the faces underneath the eyeballs. However, it would be dishonest of me to imply that I don't know their true identities. I, like many others, out of a sense of loyalty have chosen to go along with their cult of obscurity. After all, the music speaks for itself, who needs to know the names? I am also aware that it might seem somewhat strange that in a book entitled *Meet The Residents* you don't appear to do so. However, for those who can read between the lines, maybe the clues are there?

The following pages are testimony to the old adage that truth is indeed stranger than fiction. In fact, if The Residents' story were to be told as the history of some totally make-believe band, it would most probably stretch the bounds of fictional credibility, being seen as the work of an overactive imagination. However, their records exist as living proof that their story is real enough.

So settle down and prepare to meet The Residents – truly America's most eccentric band.

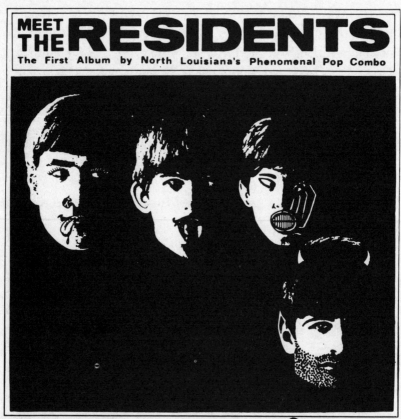

THE EARLY YEARS I

Facts about the youth of The Residents are hard to find and virtually impossible to verify. Even after 21 years, the secrecy surrounding this part of their lives remains as tight as a drum. We do know that they all hail from the deep south of America and according to the "myth"[1], they all come from Shreveport, Louisiana. One member is reputed to have come from Texas, although there is no way of verifying this fact. Best for now to stick with the myth.

Shreveport itself does exist, although it is hardly mentioned in guide books of the United States or Louisiana. It is a small place. A backwater which hardly has a scintillating history.

At the turn of the nineteenth century apart from the indians, no-one was particularly interested in Northwest Louisiana, due to the fact that it was swampy and infested with alligators and mosquitoes. However, a settlement sprang up when, in 1803, Larkin Edwards from Tennessee settled near an indian village and, after acting as an interpreter between fur traders and the local indians, was given some land.

Shreveport got its name from Henry Miller Shreve who was hired by the U.S. Government to make the Red River navigable by breaking up a huge 160 mile log jam known as the "great raft" that was blocking the river. He began his task in the Spring of 1833 with four steamboats and 159 men, completing the job in 1838. With the river and surrounding territories open to navigation the town grew and Shreveport became the seat of Caddo Parish. (Named after the Indian tribe that had originally owned the land. You can guess what happened to them.)

Nothing much exciting happened until the American Civil War when between 1863-65 Shreveport served as the wartime capital of Confederate Louisiana and its population tripled. Even then, it remained very much a backwater. Although the Confederacy was getting hammered at this time, Shreveport was only threatened with attack once and on that occasion federal troops were turned back at the battle of Mansfield. It is an historical fact that Shreveport was the last place to fly the flag of the Confederate States of America.

Since then nothing of note has really happened apart from the arrival of the railway and the modern world. Interesting, from our point of view, is the fact that in the '50s the *Louisiana Hayride* TV show was filmed in the 3,500 seater Louisiana Municipal Auditorium, mainly showcasing country talent. Two artists who were later to figure in The Residents' own recording careers got early exposure here, Hank Williams and the young Elvis Presley.

The Residents were probably too young to have witnessed Elvis strut his stuff on TV in 1954. Although no-one knows exactly when they were born, it is safe to say that they were probably only six or seven years old. However, unlike Elvis none of them were poor white trash. They have admitted to attending college. Indeed, two of them were thrown together for the first time as room-mates. From here on like most young boys they formed a loose gang of friends and this became a fraternity of five. According to Homer Flynn of the Cryptic Corporation they were, "...drawn together by the kind of "outsider" mentality. They used to tell jokes and make rude noises as part of their budding alienation."[2]

Apparently, their favourite reading material at this time was J.D.Salinger's *Catcher In The Rye*, although one of them admits that he has never read the book at all. However, the fact that they should pick on this particular book is hardly surprising. First published in 1951, the novel is an early classic tale of confused American adolescence. Like most American teenage males of the time experiencing growing pains, The Residents were probably as confused, horny and judgemental as Holden Caulfield. Maybe they were all subjected to a similar type of boarding school.

No doubt they led the lives of typical American teenagers. They resented their parents, learned to drive, double-dated, borrowed each others' clothes, took their first taste of alcohol, sex, and a conscious interest in music, especially rhythm and blues records which they bought from Stan's Record Store in Shreveport. James Brown's *Live at The Apollo* was apparently seminal in their musical education, as it was for a lot of white kids investigating the dark side of the musical spectrum at the time.

Around 1966, if we believe the myth, after two of them had made it through college they moved out to California. As Homer Flynn explains, "The South in the '60s... was not a pleasant place for anybody who had any kind of offbeat point of view about life at all. So it's not particularly hard for me to see why they were glad to get out of the South."[3] If the opportunity had presented itself they would have gone to New York, Washington, Los Angeles or any other of America's big cities. However, they went to San Francisco because one of them was already living out there. It was that simple.

They loaded up and headed west. According to legend their truck broke down some 25 miles outside of San Francisco in a small residential suburb called San Mateo. They settled here and eventually ended up en-masse in a low rent apartment above a car spraying business. The paint fumes would seep up through the floorboards.

They did not immediately embark upon their musical experiments. At this time the hippy movement was beginning to flower in California and was embraced wholeheartedly by these artistic young men from the strictly conformist background of Louisiana. They grew their hair, took all manner of drugs, got heavily into Jazz, Captain Beefheart, Frank Zappa and other "head" bands, no doubt indulging in as much free love as they could get their hands on.

To finance their existence they got jobs. One unloaded luggage from commercial airliners and was a source of amusement amongst the others, because in order to keep his job, he had to keep his hair short. The others either sold insurance or worked in a medical facility in some capacity or other.

They began to indulge their artistic natures. Producing silkscreens, painting, and even taking "arty" photographs of themselves posing naked in boxcars on the railway sidings next to their apartment. At this time in their lives, the embryonic Residents were apparently more interested in exposure than obscurity. They even threw a party for one of their girlfriends dressed in nothing but their birthday suits.

Their musical activities were probably a natural extension of their interest in the progressive music of the time, being inspired to make their own music by bands they saw at the Fillmore West and the records they bought. Perhaps at this early stage they even considered attempting to form a band in the traditional sense. Allocating instruments – bass, drums, guitar and vocals – and learning to play them. Perhaps that was the last thing they wanted to do. Maybe they just wanted to have some fun. Just make some noise – as none of them were competent musicians. Just a bunch of hippy guys![4]

Footnotes.
1. Matt Groening in *The Official WEIRD Book of The Residents,* 1981.
2. *Berkeley Barb*, Sept 8-14th, 1978
3. Ibid.
4. In correspondence to me, The Residents would like it to be known that they do not have long hair, wear tie dies and religiously attend Grateful Dead concerts.

THE EARLY YEARS II

"Composing with a tape recorder is a fascinating new line of musical adventure. Depending on the attitude and ability of the composer (and, it must be admitted, to some extent on the amount and quality of the equipment) it can be anything from an amusing hobby to an advanced art. The musically ignorant owner of a simple tape recorder can learn to record and organise sounds into real compositions, and gain much pleasure in the process. The enthusiast who can afford a more elaborate machine, or even two, can extend his abilities much further.

Alternatively, two or more people could pool their resources. Perhaps one of the owners is particularly interested in sound equipment and is knowledgeable on the electronic and technical side, in which case he might well take on all or most of the actual recording and machine operation: another owner might be more musical and would do all the planning and making the actual sounds."[1]

From *Musique Concrete for Beginners* by Terence Dwyer

"The tape recorders were more important than the instruments."[2]

A Resident.

They began making tapes in 1970 mostly for their own amusement. The fact that they could not play any instrument other than in a most crude manner did not get in the way of this process. Even at this stage they were less interested in performing than recording. Although they only possessed rudimentary recording equipment and instruments obtained from thrift stores, this did not stop them experimenting. According to future business associate Jay Clem, "...they had something like a two-track and a single-track and they just mixed down and mixed down."[3]

The way they made music at this time was very informal. Due to the restraints of day jobs and social commitments they only jammed on Tuesday evenings and at weekends. Sometimes these sessions were structured – they might try to cover a song or work out an idea someone had brought along – on other occasions they just got stoned started to play and waited to see what happened. Another concept introduced into jam sessions was where musicians would not be allowed to play their favourite instrument; "...it would stimulate new ideas that you would never have had otherwise." Apparently at one of these sessions "Snakefinger" (Phillip Lithman) was restricted totally to trombone, which he had never touched before in his life."[4]

Lithman had his own recollections:

"When we first met we were living in this place which was divided into cubicles with bits of black plastic. After we'd jammed all day, I'd climb into my little black lagoon and they would still be at it. It was an exploratory time when we were feeling our oats, feeling the possibilities of what we could do. We put ourselves in all sorts of mental conditions – feeling fresh, tired, using drugs – to see what the outcome would be like playing under those conditions."[5]

Some of these jam sessions would be recorded and edited. None of these early recordings have seen the light of day. *Rusty Coathangers For The Doctor* was recorded in June 1970 and *The*

Ballad of Stuffed Trigger in August of the same year. Apparently they contained original material as well as a number of cover versions. They are probably simply the highlights from jam sessions and this is borne out by Jay Clem who stated that, "The first two are highly documentary in nature. Most of them consisted of conversations but there was some actual music."[6]

However, despite limited musical technique and recording apparatus, by this time they were taking their manufactured music seriously. Whatever disinformation was subsequently put out as a smokescreen in later years, they were now actively pursuing a recording contract. The next tape, recorded in September 1970, was deemed good enough to send as a demo tape to Hal Halverstadt at Warner Brothers Records, complete with cover art, track listing and liner notes. In the past Halverstadt had worked with Captain Beefheart – someone they greatly admired – and in his position as Marketing Director they hoped that he would lend a sympathetic ear.

Halverstadt mailed the tape back a few months later with a rejection as well a brief note, "AXPp - A for ariginality (sic); X for Xecution; P for Presentation; and p for Potential." Whether or not he told them to keep at it or tighten their grip on their day jobs is not documented.

The most important consequence of this encounter was that they finally acquired a name. They had sent in the tape anonymously with a return address. Halverstadt returned the tape to "The Residents". They had been toying with the idea of a name for some time – New Beatles being one of many – henceforth they decided to function under the "collective" name of The Residents Uninc.

Around this time Phillip Lithman and the mysterious Nigel Senada appear on the scene. Phillip Lithman (born London, June 17th, 1949) was an English guitarist and violinist. Greatly influenced by American blues he had played clubs in London in various obscure bands like Juniors Blues Band and Smiley with little success. He went to San Francisco to experience the hippy culture. According to Residents' mythology he was with the mysterious Nigel Senada who he had met in the forests of Bavaria recording bird songs! What is important about this possibly mythical being – who has been seen in the flesh less times than the Loch Ness Monster – was his theories about musical composition and their alleged influence upon The Residents.

Because of his inability to speak much English, there is nothing in print of Senada explaining his concept of music. There is a recording made on 30th October 1971 of a hilarious Lithman radio interview with KHSC-FM Arcata, California, where the only thing that seems to be keeping him from laughing as he relates his colleague's theory of Phonetic Organisation is the tongue in his cheek. (Senada was allegedly sitting next to him in the studio). There follows a "demonstration" by the duo, a furious performance of a piece entitled *Cantata for und saxophone und a violin*. It is less music than a free form improvisation that starts nowhere, goes nowhere and ends nowhere.

Whether Senada existed or not is a matter of speculation. However, when dealing with The Residents there is no escaping his Theory of Phonetic Organisation. Over the next ten years it was to form the cornerstone of how they allegedly approached and produced their music. Fortunately, the fact that Senada never explained it in words or print did not stop the members of The Cryptic Corporation speaking up on his behalf. Here are two explanations, firstly from *Vacation* magazine:

"Phonetic Organisation was developed at that time. The theory actually applied itself to lyric writing more than it did to the music. It was a point of view by which the contents of the words were made subordinate to the sound of the words as they put themselves together. This applied itself to the music sometimes because The Residents would write the words first, then they would try to create the music to follow the lyrics."[7]

Jay Clem picks up the story:

"Well, it's an abstract concept, rather than literal. It's like a 'phonetic spelling' approach to music; not so much a notation, more a method of playing. If you can't read music, you don't know what it's supposed to sound like, so you structure it according to how you feel it should sound. It's a more natural way of playing music."[8]

The Theory of Phonetic Organisation was in reality a smokescreen to cover up The Residents' initial lack of proficiency as musicians. That they could not play in the formal sense was demonstrated by a live performance given in October 1971 at The Boarding House in San Francisco on "Audition Night". The event was fortunately taped and allows a first peek at the Residential embryo:

"Hello Everybody, how y'all doing tonight? Well, here we are again. Got a nice little show all worked up for ya. Well, I think you're gonna like it. We got all kind of little songs for ya, gonna have a few nice dances for ya, it's just going to be a wonderful, wonderful show. Yes, yes, yes, you're just going to be crazy about it. Well, we're going to start off now with a little song all about evil and wicked spirits. You think you gonna like that? Eh? Eh? EEEEHHHHHH?[9]

The "Song" itself sounds like a group exorcism. Screams and petrified vocals. The only musical accompaniment is a tape recording of what sounds like wind or very rudimentary white noise. The song progresses into a wildly improvised saxophone solo accompanied by some circus thumping of a big bass drum. The piece ends to complete and utter silence from an obviously stunned audience. The ice is only broken by one of the performers (who sounds remarkably like Jay Clem) starting off some cheerleading mostly around the theme of "N. Senada! N. Senada!" The performance continues, with chants, more saxophone (accompanied by Lithman on violin) and a song by musical collaborator Peggy Honeydew.

The performance – clocking in at just under 15 minutes – (maybe they were afraid of being thrown off) ends to wild applause from an audience of what sounds like around 40 people. There is a photograph of this event. The tiny stage is crammed full of people and everyone has extremely long hair and is wearing sunglasses. Other pictures were taken, significantly one of Phillip Lithman playing his violin. In this picture one of his fingers seems boneless, wriggling in the air like a demented snake. One of The Residents commented upon this "Snakefinger" and Lithman believing that any decent guitar player had to have a good nickname accepted this baptism with good grace.

This performance formed part of their next demo tape which was also rejected. Entitled *Baby Sex* the cover art was a picture taken from a Danish porn magazine of a woman indulging in oral sex with a baby which was also silkscreened onto T-shirts. Significantly, portions of this tape have seen the light of day and allow us our first peek at the kind of things The Residents were producing in their San Mateo 'studio' at the time. Zappa's "King Kong" is given a rather faithful rendition by Phillip "Snakefinger" Lithman. However, "Eloise" and "Kamikaze Lady" reveal that even at this stage The Residents own peculiar trademark 'sound' was coming together. "Eloise" revolves around a fantastic multi-tracked trombone and saxophone riff over which a gruff hysterical voice delivers a lyrical poem that had been performed without music a year previously at a private party. "Kamikaze Lady" is carried by another extremely guttural Beefheartish vocal, heartbeat bass drum and all manner of rudimentary tape effects.

At the end of 1971 or very early in 1972, Phillip "Snakefinger" Lithman went back to England. The exact circumstances concerning his departure are vague although there is a tasteful silkscreened poster in existence announcing his wedding at 3pm on the 31st October 1971 (Halloween). According to sources close to the band the ceremony *did* take place. However, in keeping with the relaxed attitude of the time nobody thought about going up to the City Hall and formally notifying the relevant authorities of the Union. This may account for Lithman's sudden departure as his visa may have expired. As for the mysterious N. Senada, according to the legend he simply vanished into the thin Arctic air of Greenland.

In 1972 The Residents moved into the heart of San Francisco. They rented an extremely long rectangular two storey house in Sycamore Street in the run down Mission District. They looked at their accommodation, not as living space, but somewhere they could fully express themselves by establishing a proper and permanent studio space for their music and indulge other ideas and plans. However, at the time of this move one of them peeled away to do his own thing. It would be wrong to say that he left the band as at this time there was really not a band to speak of. He simply moved out of their artistic grouping and into something else.

It was at this stage that they decided to make a record. Their attempts to secure a record deal had floundered and so they decided that if nobody else was going to release their music then they would do it themselves.

A statement of artistic independence, *Santa Dog* was a double pack single which also served as a Christmas card and a tool to promote the music they were recording. It was, in effect, an early marketing move – a ploy to gain some attention and probably something tangible to show for the last two years of intermittent musical activity. The gatefold hand-printed *Santa Dog* cover was a silkscreen of an original photograph of a dog in Christmas clothing. The innards featured a very George Cruikshank-like drawing, illustrating the track titles with the logo "Seasons greetings – Residents Uninc". The record label was called Ralph Records – the name coming apparently from an in-joke – going outside to call Ralph which meant to vomit. Ralph was also a reference to a pet dog. Indeed, The Residents always regarded Ralph Records as their "pet" label.

The four tracks – "Fire", "Explosion", "Lightning" and "Aircraft Damage" – random names taken from an insurance policy, were each attributed to four fictional bands – Ivory and the Braineaters, Delta Nudes, The College Walkers and Arf & Omega featuring the Singing Lawn Chairs. Apparently each person in the parent organisation that was Residents Uninc had their own "band" but the membership in each was the same.

Around 500 sets of *Santa Dog* were manufactured, although damage to some of the sleeves meant that only 400 complete sets could be made up. Even then these were hardly perfect. Many of the records were packaged and shrinkwrapped before the varnish that was applied to seal the ink and give the record a glossy high quality appearance had dried. Consequently most of the gatefold sleeves were stuck together! Some 300 sets were mailed out to friends, record companies and people whom The Residents admired like Frank Zappa and President Nixon. Zappa's copy was returned – he had moved. His personalised copy was later given away in a competition. Overall, the response was hardly enthusiastic. There was certainly no record company interest and even friends took took the atonal 'Christmas' music to be a joke.

No wonder. The "music" on *Santa Dog* is extremely experimental. "Fire" is the only track that utilizes a traditional "song" structure and even this is twisted into discord. The other three tracks are a series of tape splices collaged into short sonic "suites." An obvious lack of musicianship is glossed over by sheer resourcefulness. There is a heavy reliance upon vocal orchestration; slogans, chants, conversation, screams and scraps of poetry. Percussion is either rudimentary or "sampled" from other peoples recordings. (Amado Roldan's 1930 *Concert Percussion For Orchestra* is one source. A pack of barking dogs another). The primary instrument is the tape recorder. None of these tracks could have been realised without the overdubbing techniques it allowed The Residents to utilize. The final product was disturbing, unsettling, extremely avant-garde and yet strangely compelling. Even at this early stage The Residents' music sounded unlike anything else.

Thus did The Residents recording career commence. They would not release another record on their own label for two years. In the meantime they would devote their energies to a project "advertised" on the perimeter of the gatefold sleeve of *Santa Dog*. A full length feature film.

Footnotes
1. Musique Concrete for Beginners. Terence Dwyer (Oxford) 1971
2. A Resident. The Official WEIRD Book of The Residents. (WEIRD 2nd Edition 1981)
3. Jay Clem to *Keyboard* October 1982
4. Hardy Fox to *Keyboard* October 1982
5. Philip Lithman to Lesley Sly, *Sonics*, November 1986.
6. Jay Clem to *New Musical Express* February 18th 1978.

VILENESS FATS

"Arf and Omega are the Berry Boy Twins. And when the Berry Boy Twins are not pursuing their occupation as tag-team wrestlers, they often indulge in bits of Indian occultism. This is one of those times.

Civil disorder has erupted in the small colony of Vileness Flats. Using a little Indian magic, these two conjure up an Indian Priestess to help settle this dispute. But this particular Indian priestess has a problem - she lives forever, and is always falling in love with short powerful men who quickly die."[1]

Synopsis of Vileness Fats. The Cryptic Guide to The Residents (1986).

As soon as they moved into Sycamore Street, The Residents started on their most ambitious project yet – a full length feature film. That they knew literally nothing about the complex world of film production was a minor detail. As with their music it was attempting to make reality of their ideas that was the driving force. The fact they were not musicians had not stopped them recording and releasing their own music – similarly they were not filmmakers but they would attempt their own full length feature film.

Their new accommodation was two stories high with a huge rectangular open plan ground floor that they decided to convert into a film set and recording area. They would live upstairs. Working within the limitations of space they developed a plot to fit in with their surroundings. The ceilings were eleven feet high and in order to give the illusion of space they decided to base their story in a kingdom of one-armed midgets. The kingdom was originally to be called *Vileness Flats* but it was decided to take the "L" out of the Flats.

Initially, at least, they decided to meet all the production costs. Exercising full creative control over all aspects of project, they designed and constructed the sets and costumes themselves. Although they owned a 16mm film camera (and had shot some footage with it), a decision was made to film everything in half inch black and white videotape. Perhaps film stock would have worked out as too expensive. There may have also been a problem with the amount of light required to obtain good exposure, despite the fact that they had bought some studio lights from a friend in Los Angeles for $1,000.

They settled upon videotape because they saw it as the coming medium. It also served another important function. As none of The Residents knew anything about film production, videotape would allow them to see the results of what they had filmed immediately, like playing back musical tape. Lighting and camera angles could be adjusted and retakes done straight away.

Although *Vileness Fats* was produced by The Residents, there were other people involved. Indeed, one actress played such a major role that she was at one time promised in writing 5% of any gross profits accruing from the completed film. Graeme Whifler, at that time a student in "...a crummy California film school"[2], got involved with lighting sets and even did some direction. Friends and even casual acquaintances were roped in to help out as extras. Anyone who could contribute. Even though he did not know them at the time J.Raul Brody recalls a chance telephone conversation leading to an invitation to "...come down to the studio this weekend. We'll put you in the movie." He describes the set up at Sycamore Street at this time:

> "...it was a small room that had most of their electronic gear and some instruments, acoustically retiled, and next to that... the rest of the garage was their storage for props and stuff and also the film set of *Vileness Fats*. The upstairs was the living quarters, which again is another thing that attracted me to their work. It was just more heavily decorated than anything I have ever seen in my life. I felt, these guys know what they're doing... I was just a struggling musician at the time who didn't really think about the bigger picture, these guys not only thought about the bigger picture but had an idea of the bigger picture they wanted to put out."[3]

Brody ended up as a waiter serving huge broccoli heads to the Mayor of Vileness Fats during the banquet scene. He was to later assist them on some of their recording projects.

As The Residents all had day jobs, filming took time. They could only work on *Vileness Fats* during the evenings and at weekends. Rotas were drawn up so that one person would cook each night of the week whilst the others worked downstairs. The Residents functioned as a commune at this time, pooling income to buy food, equipment, props and film stock. One of them made the ultimate sacrifice and sold his sportscar to help with the finances, photographing the $1,200 cash received. They even produced *Vileness Fats* stationery.

However, after four years the film was abandoned. What went wrong? For one thing it became increasingly obvious that the format was obsolete and there was no way the black and white videotape could could be transferred onto 35mm film stock as originally envisioned. In addition, despite all their painstaking efforts, the film was nowhere near being finished. Only 60% of the script had been filmed and that had taken up 14 hours of videotape! The fact that there was never a completed script no doubt hampered filming. Apparently dialogue would usually be written shortly before or during shooting to keep things spontaneous.

Their tiny little studio was also restrictive. Each hand-painted set had to be totally removed before another could be erected. Progress was slow. The nightclub scene took an entire year to construct and film. Functioning as a commune had not helped. Direction was general rather than specific. No-one was in overall control. Decisions were made collectively and therefore progress was "...slowed and denuded by the number of discussions over what should be done, what was desired and what was to be accomplished."[4] The project was officially abandoned in February 1976 after their second LP *The Third Reich and Roll* was released.

In later years, as The Residents' success grew, the failure of *Vileness Fats* became woven into the tapestry of myth and legend surrounding the band. Photographs adorned album sleeves and promotional material gave fans tantalising glimpses of what might or might not have existed. Ironically, the very technology that led to its abandonment allowed it to twitch somewhat back to life. In 1984 video enhancement allowed some of the better footage to finally see the light of day. Of course, what was released on the thirty minute videotape *Whatever Happened To Vileness Fats?* was hardly representative of the film but it does allow us a glimpse at what went on in that studio during those four years.

The video focussed upon the subplot of Arf and Omega, the Berry Boy, Siamese twin, tag wrestling team, from their arrival in Vileness Fats up until their death in a nightclub. There is no audible dialogue on the revised version, only The Residents' freshly recorded soundtrack which makes any attempt to follow what is going on quite confusing.

However, as a visual spectacle, even in black and white, the video is overwhelming. The sets and costumes are stunning, especially the interior of "The Cave" which is a womb of black balloons. Whatever the technical shortcomings on show – and there are many – there is no doubting the amount of effort that went into creating this strange and compelling surrealistic world. Cinematic technique ranges from the laughable to the slickly professional. No opportunity is wasted to fill the camera with strong visual imagery. The Residents really did create their own little world inside what was literally no more than an oversized garage.

The highlight is undoubtedly the nightclub scene. It opens with The Residents performing an original piece from the *Baby Sex* tapes entitled "Eloise". Trombones, trumpets and an accordion are played by three men in silver masks and black tuxedos and there is an exuberant performance from what can loosely be termed "the singing Resident". This sets the scene for the arrival of Arf and Omega who enjoy the warbled vocals of the following act – the blonde Peggy Honeydew – so much that they invite her to sit at their table. Much the worse for wear from drink, the twins fall into quarrelling over her affections. After much armwrestling, Honeydew produces two swords and they fight to the death watched by the nightclub crowd which includes all manner of strangely attired patrons. Arf kills Omega and therefore himself. The film was intended to be a musical comedy.

Footnotes
1. Synopsis of Vileness Fats. *The Cryptic Guide to The Residents*. (1986).
2. *Record* Magazine. October 1985.
3. J.Raul Brody. Interview with Author. October 1992
4. John Kennedy. Interview with Author. October 1992.

Who the hell are The Residents...? 2

Cartoon by Savage Pencil from Rock and Roll Zoo

MEET THE RESIDENTS

"The ideal equipment is a three-speed stereo machine with facilities for sound-on-sound, synchro, echo mixing and monitoring; plus a second machine which may be a simple mono recorder. A pair of extension speakers and a pair of stereo headphones are desirable though not essential...The reader is also warned that to try tape composition he will need much enthusiasm and patience, for he will be embarking on a very time consuming activity, and he should not do so unless he is as likely to enjoy the manufacturing process involved as the final result. (This is true of all musical composition, however.) The reader is also encouraged to believe that creative results can be achieved by the use of imagination and self-criticism, and that no great musical or technical knowledge is essential."[1]

From *Musique Concrete for Beginners* by Terence Dwyer.

"We heard that George or Ringo had a copy of *Meet The Residents* but who the fuck knows?"[2]

Jay Clem.

Although *Vileness Fats* took up a lot of time and energy, The Residents still found time to make and record music in their home studio aptly nicknamed "El Ralpho" in deference to one of their many influences; the fantastic iconoclastic Jazz/Free/Space music composer Sun Ra, who called his studios and record label El Saturn. His studio's name was based around his own personal mythology, part of which included him claiming to have come from Saturn.

In his lifetime, the late Sun Ra possessed a criminally overlooked talent, but nonetheless still managed to release over 115 LP's mainly on his own self-financed label, maintaining a cosmic band – the Arkestra – for nearly forty years. His music is a rich melange of big band swing jazz, exotic rhythm, space-age effects, personal mythology and extreme beauty. The Residents were undoubtedly influenced by him and owned a number of his LP's, as well as having checked out some of his spectacularly theatrical performances. Some of the tracks on the recent Evidence CD re-issues of his early work are very Residential sounding. These tracks with their ragged horns and quirky time signatures were recorded live between 1956 - 61!

On 1st April, 1974, The Residents released their first long playing record aptly entitled *Meet The Residents* on their own Ralph Records label. According to Jay Clem:

> "They worked on the tapes which later became the record just to take breaks from the filming. They never thought it would become a record. Later when they realised that it was going to be released they added some extra material."[3]

Meet The Residents was The Residents first real musical manifesto. Despite the decidedly poor audio quality – the record was in mono – the music laid down the firm foundations of what was to become The Residents' trademark sound. Textured, multi-tracked organic progression, ragged punchy horns, with a tremendous variety of instrumentation and orchestral percussive effects. A gumbo of vocal styles. A fascination with various time signatures. However, unlike *Santa Dog*, the music on *Meet The Residents* is much more confident in both structure and composition.

The range of material is fantastic, from the opening avant-garde cover version of "These Boots Are Made For Walking" to the beautiful multi-tracked piano textures of the neo-classical "Rest Aria". "Smelly Tongues" is all frantic guitar. The repetitive two note wailing and spoken narrative of "Skratz" is hypnotic. "Spotted Pinto Bean" is an early experiment with operatic effects. "Infant Tango" is a funky sub James Brown mixture of wah wah guitar, bass and drums punctuated by what was to become trademark multi-tracked Residential horns, inspired by Stan Kenton (not unsurprising considering his 1950s experimentation), Henry Mancini, Sun Ra and Prez "Mambo King" Prado. "Seasoned Greetings" is relaxed, confident and stately with a slight tinge of jazz. There is also humour, the Human Beinz' "Nobody but Me" being played, stuck in a groove and then "treated." "N-R-GEE (Crisis Blues)" is a driving, forceful musical and gutteral vocal rant. The album closes with a slowly fading chorus chant of "Go home America, fifty five'll do." A direct comment upon the thousands of American casualties during the Vietnam war.

As with the *Santa Dog* double single, tremendous effort went into the packaging. The Residents wanted to make a statement upon contemporary music as well as to present a strong arresting image that might invite random purchase. They settled upon the most iconoclastic thing they could think of; an "artistic" defacing of the *Meet The Beatles* LP, changing the logo to *Meet The Residents*. The liner notes on the back were pure hype and self-promotion inviting the reader into the realms of Phonetic Organisation, N. Senada and *Vileness Fats*.

Again, they put up their own money to master and manufacture 1,050 copies of the record, although around 200 copies were deemed unusable due to warpage. Selling it was a different proposition. As an independent record company they had no way of distributing the record and getting it accepted in record shops. As they had no interest (or ability) to promote their music by live performance they had to explore alternatives. They decided to try and stir interest by the novel idea of manufacturing some some 4,000 8" clear flexi-discs which contained seven minutes of music from the album. These "samplers" would be given away free and hopefully encourage sales.

Subsequently, a full page advertisement was taken out in the February 1974 issue of the Canadian art publication *File* Magazine that included a copy of the flexidisc and offered the LP for $1.99. However, there was a general belief that the advertisement – featuring the defaced Beatles – was an elaborate joke. This was no doubt enhanced by poor distribution and the atonal music that greeted listeners of the disc, and as a result there was not one single response.

Unpeturbed, they advertised in *Friday* (May 17th, 1974) a free magazine distributed amongst all of San Francisco's colleges. Again, the LP sleeve was prominently displayed and an advertisement offered "Free samples" of the record and a contact telephone number. Free copies were also given away in the magazine's competition.

Again the response was not overwhelming. Apparently, in the first year of release only some 40 people bought the album of their own free will. When a record store (Rather Ripped records in Berkeley) finally took a few copies, The Residents were so overjoyed they went down and took photographs of one prominently displayed in the record rack.

The fact that *Meet The Residents* hardly sold upon first being released is not surprising. At the time of its release, ear friendly bands like The Osmonds and the Jackson 5 were dominating the airwaves. Even progressive music fans would have found *Meet The Residents* unpalatable. It was more extremely experimental than anything Zappa, Pink Floyd or even the like-minded studio-based German collective Faust had produced. The music defied catagorisation. It was not rock, not jazz, not contemporary classical, although there were elements of all three in the music.

It was a totally new sound, indeed an entirely new approach to music. There was no interest in being a "band", writing songs, playing them live and then recording them. The Residents were simply interested in the possibilities offered by the recording process itself and constructing their music piece by piece on tape. If any review copies were sent out to music magazines they were not reviewed and radio airplay was simply out of the question even for the more "open eared" college circuit.

The idea of a promotional flexi disc was a good one but perhaps a double edged sword. Those people who did take the trouble to play it, probably did not take too kindly to the atonal explosion that leapt out of their speakers. The flexi, rather than gaining sales, probably lost them. Then again, at least those few people who did buy the record knew what they were letting themselves in for.

Tom Timony, later to work for Ralph Records, recalls his first experience of their music:

"I got turned onto The Residents in 1975 in France. Someone had a *Meet The Residents* record and hated it. I was into progressive music and they said that I might like it. It was so minimal. I hated it... I thought they were so primitive. They didn't know anything about music. As a musician you could tell that they had something that most musicians never have, which is that savvy for timbres and things... all these exotic sounds and different time signatures that in traditional music are not supposed to happen."[4]

Of course, nothing did happen. Apart from a few "dedicated fools" the world was not yet ready to embrace the music of The Residents.

Footnotes
1. Musique Concrete for Beginners. Terence Dwyer. (Oxford 1971) Page 2.
2. Vacation., Spring 1981 (In fact, one member of the Cryptic Corporation had actually given John Lennon a copy of the LP.)
3. Vacation. Spring 1981.
4. Tom Timony. Interview with the Author October 1992.

THIRD REICH AND ROLL

"The only valid art can be done truly in obscurity. Only if the artist is working by himself and for his satisfaction, without any knowledge of the world to influence him, can he come out with something pure for himself, pure art. The theory has had a tremendous influence on The Residents."[1]

"The two things they really enjoy doing are creating music that nobody has ever heard before and then taking other people's music and making it sound like music that nobody has ever heard before."[2]

Homer Fynn

When *Meet The Residents* failed to sell like hot cakes, The Residents threw their energies and financial resources into *Vileness Fats*. They also conveniently developed their theory of obscurity. To be frank they didn't have to work too hard at it, they *were* obscure. They had released a double single and an entire LP's worth of material to the worst kind of response of all; indifference. Therefore, why not take this obscurity to the furthest extreme possible? Record an entire LP and then announce that it was "Not Available". This is what The Residents apparently did in 1974, stating that the record could only be released once they had forgotten about its existence. Of course, this did not stop them stirring interest by mentioning that the LP was "Not Available" in the liner notes of their "third" LP *The Third Reich and Roll*.

Unlike *Meet The Residents* which was a low fidelity realisation of their own music, *The Third Reich and Roll* was a "concept" album. The Residents were highly interested in what the American music press termed the "Krautrock" phenomenon; progressive German bands like Can, Neu! Tangerine Dream, Amon Düül II, Kraftwerk and Faust and the innovative, adventurous and spirited music they were making. Jay Clem:

> *"Third Reich and Roll* was an attempt to treat Top 40 rock and roll from the '60s as if it were avant-garde material as performed by early '70s progressive German bands."[3]

The entire LP was recorded in two weeks, a year apart, in late October 1974 and October 1975. The reason for this is simple; The Residents took vacation time from their day jobs to work on the project. Of course, although most of the material was recorded in these two weeks there is no doubting that they worked on the tapes before releasing the LP. When it came to recording the music a large part was taped by laying down the original song as the first track and then The Residents built up overdubs of themselves playing along with it. Finally, the "original" version was erased from the tape leaving only the Residents "new" interpretation.

When their own musicianship was not up to scratch they simply roped in people competent enough to play the parts they required. People like Gary Phillips:

> "I was working one night at Rather Ripped (records)... somebody called and asked if there was a guitar player who could add a part to their record... I walked into this big warehouse and somebody asked me did I know "Hey Jude". I said, "sure", and he asked me if I

knew "Sympathy For The Devil", I said "sure" again and he said that was all they wanted me to play on the end of their record. I got my portable tape recorder and plugged into that. I didn't even use an amplifier. All I can remember is these enormous sponge rubber broccolis lying around everywhere. They looked exactly like the real thing – right shape, right colour and everything – only they were bigger than me!"[4]

Third Reich and Roll is one of the cornerstones upon which The Residents' reputation is based. It is a dense collage of sounds, totally alien yet at the same time naggingly familiar. The music is divided into two suites – "Hitler was a Vegetarian" and "Swastikas on Parade". Each is a tapestry made up of a number of covered '60s hits. "Land of 1,000 Dances", "Wipe Out", "Sunshine of Your Love", "96 Tears", "It's My Party", "Light My Fire", "Pushing Too Hard", "Good Lovin", "Gloria", "Hey Jude" and "Sympathy For The Devil" are some of the songs gutted, deconstructed or given Residential interpretations. James Brown's "Sex Machine" is even plundered for a sample.

There is a tremendous amount of playful iconoclasm about the music. For example, the short version of "Light My Fire" sounds as if it were recorded by a man riding a galloping horse. "The Twist" starts off with German lyrics and then dissolves into a fantastic mutation of "Land of a 1,000 Dances". The music itself almost defies description. A phenomenal amount of instruments are used – saxophones, trombones, guitar, bass, koto, accordion, oud, pipe organ and xylophone to name a few. There is also the first trademark use of synthesisers – an Arp Odyssey and a rented Arp string ensemble bubble and scratch accompaniment on both sides – seen to best effect on "Good Lovin" where it contributes some noodling Sun Ra-like effects. Of course, the main instrument on show is The Residents' mastery of their recently acquired Tascam eight track recording equipment and a battery of effects – reverb, echo and distortion – and the way that they construct and mix the music. In one fantastic sequence helicopters buzz between the speakers, cars crash, gunfire breaks out and eerie music rises out of the mix like the creature from the black lagoon.

The cover art was as shocking as the music. Taking the German connection to its logical extreme, a smiling cartoon-like Dick Clark – host of "American Bandstand", the '60s rock programme of American TV – he is pictured in full Nazi uniform, smiling, holding a hand-coloured carrot surrounded by dancing teenage Hitlers. The design along with the black, red and grey colouring is totally arresting. The back cover featured a large germanic emblem with a swastika inside. Liner notes were folded around the record sleeve.

As with *Meet The Residents*, 1,000 copies were pressed and officially released. Promotional pictures were taken featuring The Residents wearing huge swastikas on their heads. These pictures were banned when hung in Rather Ripped Records in Berkeley. Despite this The Residents found that there was a market for their record, not a floodgate but a definite interest in their product. In the preceding two years *Meet The Residents* had slowly begun to sell and they had acquired a small cultish underground following.

To promote themselves and the record they even went as far as to perform on 7th June, 1976, at Rather Ripped Records' fifth birthday party in Berkeley. It was a performance event more than a concert entitled; *Oh Mummy! Oh Daddy! Can't You See That It's True: What The Beatles Did To Me. "I Love Lucy" Did To You.* The promoter recalls:

"It was rather difficult, we didn't know who these people were... I don't think audiences were ready for this sort of thing... we hold ourselves to be pretty progressive here in Berkeley but I really don't think that could be called entertaining... they arrived with a lot of scaffolding and by the time they had finished you could hardly see anything anyway and as for the music – well, I'm not sure there was any music... I like to see who I'm dealing with and these people were all wearing fencing masks..."[5]

The performance was meticulously planned. 16mm excerpts from *Vileness Fats* and other footage (which would later become the *Third Reich and Roll* promotional video) was shown. The set list gave running times for the songs as well as stage direction due to the fact that a large portion of the music was not played "live" but pre-recorded onto backing tapes. There were a host of collaborators, including Zeibak and Peggy Honeydew who had also contributed vocals to *Third Reich and Roll*. More importantly the concert also featured the recently returned Phillip "Snakefinger" Lithman – dressed as an artichoke – on guitar.

Lithman had moved to Los Angeles in 1976 and taken up permanent residence in San Francisco in 1978. However, he had not been idle during his time in England(1972-76) forming Chilli Willi and the Red Hot Peppers with friend Martin Stone. As well as playing a legion of live performances, they recorded and released two LP's – *Kings of the Robot Rhythm* (1974) and *Bongos Over Balham* (1975). A third LP was supposed to be released on Stiff Records in 1976/7 (with vibrator art by Edwin Pouncey aka Savage Pencil) but this never materialised. The music on these two LP's sounds nothing like Lithman's later work. It is mellow country blues with twangy guitar and bar-room violin. Both sound as if they had been recorded in America rather than England.

For the concert, The Residents themselves performed a truncated version of a new work – "Six Things To a Cycle" – behind a net curtain swathed from head to foot in surgical bandages. It looked good but made playing difficult. As one of them later related to *Future* fanzine...; "Unfortunately, we had not tried playing while wearing the costumes in advance... We're still trying to figure out what we did."[6]

The concert was taped and features a short version of what was to become their next single. The Residents had contemplated releasing a single from the *Third Reich and Roll* LP. "Gloria" or "Good Lovin" may have been considered. However, they finally decided to cover one more song and invest it with everything that had gone into the making of the LP. The chosen stalking horse was the Rolling Stones' classic "Satisfaction".

Additional musicians were drafted in. Phillip "Snakefinger" Lithman and The Pointless Sisters; "They needed extra singers for "Satisfaction" which they were just about to record and asked (us) to do the back up vocals."[7]

The resulting single was later to be described by a critic from *Trouser Press* Magazine as "the most determinedly repellent music I have ever heard, guaranteed to empty a room inside of 10 or 15 seconds." It is without doubt the most extreme of all The Residents' recordings. Whilst the songs on *Third Reich and Roll* are covered with humour, "Satisfaction" is simply gunned down and murdered. Everything is totally overloaded. The vocals are screamed and rendered into almost incoherent feedback by electronic treatment. Snakefinger brings what was to become his sonic trademark guitar to bear. As for The Pointless Sisters' back-up vocals, they were so bad they were edited out of the final mix. "Satisfaction" is raw bleeding music, challenging the listener to respond by either enduring or turning it off.

"Satisfaction" was to become a Residential sleeper although only two hundred were manufactured and shrink wrapped in hand-coloured sleeves. It was marketed as a collector's item. There was even a card inside to be returned to Ralph Records so that the purchaser could be kept informed of the subsequent increase (if any) in value.

The Schwump single, released at the same time as "Satisfaction" is a real oddity. Around 1975 on a trip to Portland Oregon, one of The Residents met the mysterious Schwump. He had his own radio show and was partial to featuring his full length frog opera on air. A visiting Resident heard this and invited him to San Francisco and started recording material for a proposed album to be released on Ralph Records. However, Schwump was somewhat worried that people might rip off his original material and so at first liked the idea of the single being released in a limited edition of 200 copies. Then his position turned around 180 degrees and he suggested to The Residents that they were not pressing enough records to give his genius the exposure it deserved! Eventually, he vanished.

Compared to "Satisfaction", "Aphids in the Hall/You're a Martian/Home" is very straight-laced. Indeed, "Aphids" sounds like a few guys having fun. It is very straight ahead and swings like a tune from a old Broadway show. "You're a Martian" is more of the same with a nicely whistled opening. Only "Home" is Residential. This is one of the rarest Residents' records. It has never been re-released in any form.

In 1993, Schwump re-established contact with The Residents by completing and returning the "collectors" card which had been inside his personal copy of "Aphids" for nearly 20 years.

Footnotes
1. Homer Flynn to *Berkeley Barb* October 8 1978.
2. Ibid.
3. Jay Clem to *Berkeley Barb*, October 8th 1978
4. Gary Phillips to *Sounds* 13th May 1978
5. Rather Ripped Records promoter.
6. Future fanzine (no.2) New York 1977.
7. Interview with Author. October 1992.

Who the hell are The Residents... ? 3

Cartoon by Savage Pencil from Rock and Roll Zoo

THE CRYPTIC CORPORATION

"The bureaucracy is there because it's necessary in the music business at present – which is not to say it doesn't have some symbolic significance."[1]

Jay Clem.

"The work that I have been doing these many years parallels much in the attitudes and actions of primitive man. He found sound-magic in the common materials around him. He then proceeded to make the vehicle, the instrument, as visually beautiful as he could. Finally, he involved the sound magic and the visual beauty in his everyday words and experiences, his ritual and drama, in order to lend greater meaning to his life. This is my trinity: sound-magic, visual beauty, experience ritual."[2]

Taken from sleevenotes of The Music of Harry Partch

The two hundred hand-printed "Satisfaction" singles were all numbered and signed "Goodbye Residents Uninc". This did not refer to the demise of the band and record label but a radical change in "business" structure. Henceforth there would no longer just be The Residents and Ralph Records. There would also be The Cryptic Corporation.

The Cryptic Corporation were four "friends" who wanted to manage and promote The Residents. More importantly, one of the Corporation – John Kennedy – had just inherited a substantial amount of money and was prepared to sink some of this into supporting and promoting The Residents. The other three placed some equity into the venture but The Cryptic Corporation was formed mainly to protect his financial stake. (If the business had remained a partnership any creditor could legally target the individual with most money; ie. Kennedy).

Today, an athletic looking man in his mid-forties, Kennedy is keen to stress that, "I wasn't a Resident. The Residents did the recordings."[3] He simply bankrolled the whole affair.

The four officers of The Cryptic Corporation each assumed roles. Kennedy himself became President with special responsibility for Production and Administration, Business School graduate Jay Clem became the Business Manager and Publicist, Homer Flynn assumed responsibility for graphic design and Hardy Fox used his knowledge of sound engineering the assist The Residents in realising their projects.

The first act of The Cryptic Corporation was to buy a building – 444 Grove Street – in an area of San Francisco known as Hays Valley. Today, the area is moving steadily upmarket and is only a five minute walk from the downtown Civic Centre. Back in 1976 however, the area was low rent, run down and divided from the Civic Centre by the busy South Freeway that ran right alongside the party wall of 444 Grove Street. The motel across the street was a favourite place for prostitutes to entertain clients.

When the Cryptics first arrived to inspect the property with a view to purchase, the first thing they saw was a fresh bullethole in the door. Inside, there were holes in the roof. This did not deter them. The building was ideal for their needs. Double fronted with a large warehouse to one side and offices on the other. There was also a house included in the price. More importantly, "We could afford it. It was cheap." It cost $100,000. "We bought the building and provided it."[4]

The Residents gleefully moved into their new business premises although they never lived there. Even though *Vileness Fats* had been abandoned they brought along all the sets and costumes, all of their musical equipment as well as their huge record collection which they often rifled through for ideas. Chris Cutler argues in his excellent chapter on The Residents in his book *File Under Popular* (ReR Megacorp 1991 Edition) that The Residents sound developed "not from a knowledge of the various (musical) 'rules' of construction, but from a highly developed listening familiarity".[5] This theory certainly holds some water in the early part of their career, especially *Third Reich*, "Six Things to a Cycle", "Satisfaction" and "Flying". Indeed, one source interviewed for this book recalls them listening intently as late as 1981 to the music of the soundtrack composer Ennio Morriocone to work out just how he put his music together.

Grove Street was redesigned. Graeme Whifler, a film-maker friend, constructed a large mural on the front of the building and metal trees were added onto the front door. As for the inside:

> "...one passes through the hallway lined in blue plastic, past the Mickey Mouse statue, stacks of record boxes, a gigantic version of the RCA dog, and up the circular stairway adorned with mummified baby dolls hung from the bannister with hangmen's nooses, and into the corporate loft..."[6]

Now that they had their own building to work from and "business support", The Residents all gave up their day jobs to concentrate full-time upon their music and related activities. Whether their day-to-day existence was sponsored by The Cryptic Corporation is a grey area. They were certainly not living on the money generated by record sales. At this time they were merely a very small cult band and as late as February 1977 were still offering for sale copies of "Satisfaction" and "Aphids in The Hall" which had been limited to a pressing of 200 singles each.

As to what The Cryptic Corporation expected to get for such a significant investment in what was, "a far corner of the art world"[7] is a matter of speculation. American business is notorious for not sponsoring fledgling art. The Residents were no McDonalds' franchise. Perhaps the Cryptics had a crystal ball. Perhaps they were The Residents themselves...

Whatever, under this new regime there was a flurry of activity. Whereas previously "The Residents as art commune" had been reticent to market themselves, The Cryptic Corporation had no such scruples. In February 1977, in an effort to boost sales, the first Ralph Records mail order catalogue appeared offering all of the Residents' records for sale, as well as T-shirts featuring the iconoclastic *Meet The Residents* cover. There was even a special limited edition *Third Reich and Roll* collector's boxed set on offer. There was also the inducement of a new LP; *Fingerprince*.

Fingerprince is in many respects a transitional release. Revealing the true depth of The Residents' musical divergence. One entire side of the LP was given over to "Six Things To a Cycle", a piece inspired by Indonesian Gamelan and the challenging repetitive music of minimalist composers Phillip Glass, Steve Reich and Terry Riley.

However, the main influence was the obscure maverick composer Harry Partch. Like themselves, Partch (born Oakland, California, 24th June 1901) developed his career outside of the mainstream. Rejecting Western scales and classical techniques,

Partch looked to Africa and the Far East for inspiration and therefore his music is extremely rhythmic in nature. Partch developed his own 43 note scale, "modified" existing instruments as well as building his own – the Harmonic Canon III, Cloud Chamber Bowls and the fantastically named Whang-gun (it makes a "whang" sound) to name but a few.

Partch recruited and trained his own Gate 5 Ensemble to play these instruments and perform and record his own compositions. In one instance he recorded a film score by himself by multi-tracking all the instruments himself (Windsong 1958). He ploughed his furrow in obscurity, funding his existence by live performances, various short-lived teaching and research posts, and sales of his music through his own Gate 5 record label. Recognition came only in his final years.

On "Six Things To a Cycle", The Residents play normal, found and self-constructed instruments like a mahogany xylophone. The long rhythmic suite of music tells a story; in this case, how "man, represented by a primitive humanoid, is consumed by his self-created environment only to be replaced by a newer creature, still primitive, still faulty, but destined to rule the world just as poorly."[8] The piece is beautifully realised from the opening jungle sounds to the screamed "birth" of man and the subsequent unravelling of the music. There is humour too. A long rhythmic chorus around the theme of "Chew chew gum, chew gum gum...". "Six Things To a Cycle" is beautiful music and another twist of the Residential tail revealing their interest in the cutting edge of American contemporary classical music as well as their willingness to experiment with non-Western forms, structures and instrumentation. Reference was made to the fact that "Six Things To A Cycle" had been commissioned as a ballet to be performed at the Museum of Modern Art in San Francisco, but was never performed. In fact, this was part of a planned collaboration with the art-architecture group Ant Farm – notorious for their cadillac desert art structures – which never came to fruition.

Of course, "Six Things To a Cycle" was only the second side of *Fingerprince*. The first side was a collection of shorter, more typically Residential pieces. Odd socks. All are excellent, especially the two fantastic versions of "You Yesyesyes". At this time The Residents were still not fully competent musicians. Just listen to one of them struggling to play the guitar part on the second version of "You Yesyesyes Again". Also there was "Godsong" with its lyric that states that, "All that God wanted to be was just a normal deity." The 58 second "March de la Winni" was composed as the soundtrack for the opening credits of the soon to be completed *Third Reich and Roll* promotional film.

Fingerprince was supposed to be a three-sided LP. (In fact, it was originally to be titled "Tourniquet of Roses" but there was a last minute change of mind). However, the idea was abandoned due to prohibitive costs and it was decided that the missing "side" would only be included as a 7" EP in the limited edition 25 "Fingerprince" artistic boxed sets advertised in the first mail order catalogue. The boxed set was later abandoned and the small batch of EP's were sent out with refunds to the dedicated few who had sent in their money. The *Babyfingers* EP was finally released as a parting shot by The Residents first short-lived fan club (WEIRD) in 1981. One of the tracks on this EP was entitled "Death In Barstow", a subtle reference to the death of Harry Partch on the 3rd of September, 1976.

Fingerprince was evidence again, that The Residents defied categorisation. They were making their innovative music to satisfy themselves rather than market forces. Like Partch before them, they stayed true to their art despite having struggled beneath the light of obscurity.

Of course, it didn't pay the rent and therefore with a view to generating much needed cashflow from other sources, the Cryptics began exploring the possibility of opening their own movie theatre. Indeed, they even "procured property" – an "ugly grey theatre" at 11th and Howard. The idea behind this "Science Fiction and Fantasy Theatre" was:

> "for the institution of entertainment facilities for both film and live show attractions. The design and format of operation are to express a heavily fantasy-orientated point of view. Besides plans for Science Fiction and Horror film festivals, The Residents are said to be writing a show for the facility to be presented in late 1977."[9]

Before all of this could get off the ground there was a small matter of city law to attend to. Movie theatres had to provide sufficient parking space for patrons. However, if this was not possible, potential owners had to demonstrate that there was enough off street parking in the surrounding area to cope with the custom and obtain a variance in this law.

The Cryptics thought that this would not be a problem as the surrounding area was mainly industrial and there was plenty of free parking space. Therefore they assumed that all they had to do was turn up on the day of the hearing and obtain the variance. However, when local residents heard of the plans they believed that as the Cryptics had been so secretive about the whole thing, they were intending to open a hardcore gay porno cinema. The local community mobilised itself against this and raised petitions and objections to the variance being granted. The Cryptics attempted to explain their real purpose – splatter movies and aliens with two heads from outer space – but no-one would believe them. Plans were shelved in June 1977. "When questioned about the project's demise, Cryptic President John Kennedy explained that, superficially, the project cost had exceeded its earning potential... Something had to go, so obviously it had to be the theatre."[10]

The first mail order catalogue was such a success that to cope with demand it had to be reprinted in April 1977. By this time the 200 copies of "Satisfaction" and "Aphids in the Hall" and the remaining copies of "Santa Dog" had all been snapped up. The Residents also contributed a track – "Whoopy Snorp" – to an otherwise apalling avant-garde compilation album – *Blorp Esette* – released by the Los Angeles Free Music Society.[11] Word was slowly spreading outside and was no doubt assisted by features in various fanzines that sprang up in the wake of the slowly emerging "punk" scene in New York and San Francisco.

Desperate for publicity and recognition, The Residents even allowed themselves to be interviewed by the New York fanzine *Future* and a sympathetic journalist from *Friday* magazine. These interviews are often hilarious:

> A Resident, "I will say that our music tends to polarise people." Another Resident: (Chuckle) "Yeah, they love it or they hate it. But that's all to the good. At least they're reacting, even if they send us threatening letters. You can sleep your way through most of the records on the market today."[12]

Maybe one of the reasons The Residents stopped giving interviews was because they could not stop talking! However, it is certain that this policy of Perestroika was soon abandoned as it was felt that it destroyed the mystique that was slowly building up around the band.

To stoke this interest *Meet The Residents* was re-mastered for stereo, thus loosing 7 minutes of music in the process. The re-released record featured a new shellfish sleeve due to apparent legal representation from Capitol, The Beatles' American record label, over the original cover art. One wonders if this was hype. On the 1977 re-release the original defaced Beatles' LP cover still appeared on the back of the record sleeve. Also, in later years Ralph Records was to fully revert to the original sleeve for further re-issues and the *Meet The Residents* CD.

In any event The Residents' response to this legal action, real or otherwise, was musical. They released another limited edition single of 500 copies appropriately enough entitled *The Beatles play The Residents and The Residents play The Beatles*. This was offered for sale in the second Ralph Records mail order catalogue of August 1977.

This, without doubt, is one of the most perfect of all Resident releases. It encapsulates everything that they stood for being witty, spiteful, irreverent and totally original. The A side – "Beyond the Valley of a Day in The Life" – is not a song but a Frankenstein-like composition made up of various portions of songs recorded by The Beatles. It is an absolutely wicked pastiche and jarringly unmusical. The effort involved in recording, treating and making all the disparate parts gel together must have been tremendous. However, it was well worth it and the result is classic Residents; as Jon Savage put it "A terrifying dehumanised/eerie/hallucinatory collage..."[13] The "B" side is The Residents' version of "Flying" and is equally as good. They even "cover" the looped John Lennon speech from the A side – "Please, everybody we didn't do everything we could have done but we tried" – on "Flying" it is screamed with stoned laughing gleeful scorn.

The packaging for this single was again exemplary of Poreknowgraphics' (the graphic arm of the Cryptic Corporation) unique style. The Residents pose naked, arms aloft, their faces hidden by fake John, Paul, George and Ringo Beatle masks. They appear androgenous as only their pubic hair is visible. This effect was obtained not by airbrushing out their genitals, but by pulling them back between their legs and keeping them out of sight by a judicious use of string. Five pink hand-coloured shadowy fan-like hands reach out to attempt to touch them.

In a short space of time, life would imitate art and people would reach out to embrace the music of The Residents.

Footnotes

1. Jay Clem to *New Musical Express* 18th February 1978
2. Harry Partch to Composers Recordings, Inc. taken from sleevenotes of The Music of Harry Partch (CRI CD7000).
3. John Kennedy. Interview with Author. October 1992.
4. Ibid.
5. Chris Cutler in *File Under Popular* (ReR Megacorp 1991 Edition) Page 76.
6. *San Jose Mercury News* (Tab supplement) Page 4.
7. John Kennedy. Interview with Author October 1992.
8. *Fingerprince* sleevenotes.
9. Ralph Records catalog no. 1 - April 1977. Page 1.
10. Ralph Records catalog no. 2 - August 1977. Page 1.
11. There was also a single The Residents by the aptly named Slimy Adenoid and the Pablums. Like Satisfaction and Aphids it too was released in an limited art edition of 200 copies. Suffice to say the cover was better than the music.
12. *Friday Magazine*. 3rd November 1978. It should be noted that The Residents deny that this, or any other Residents interview, quoted within this book happened at all.
13. Jon Savage. *Sounds*, 26th November 1977. Page 31.

DUCK STAB

"NOT FOR the faint hearted. Be warned. Residents specialise in cultural sabotage, sonic rearrangement, cryptic capers. They are (at the same time) very funny and vary(sic) scary."[1]

Jon Savage

"..."Satisfaction", when I first heard it, was responsible for the complete re-evaluation (and savage depletion) of my record collection; which may seem more like a warning than a recommendation, but only if your tastes are static and nostalgia-based."[2]

Andy Gill

The catalyst for the growth of interest in The Residents was not their own marketing strategies but the English music press who discovered them with a vengeance in 1977/8.

Up until this time there is no doubting that The Residents had built up a small cultish American following, but this retarded cancer grew slowly through word of mouth and a few sympathetic local journalists and college radio stations. Records sold slowly and in quantities that generated the barest trickle of cashflow. The establishment of The Cryptic Corporation, the acquisition of 444 Grove Street and fancy headed stationery gave the impression of health and vitality, but in truth there was little apart from the hyperbole of the first two Ralph Records mail order catalogues printed in February/August 1977 to suggest a bright future.

However, a musical revolution was taking place across the Atlantic in England; punk rock. The heyday of the punk movement, encapsulated in the brief career of the Sex Pistols (1976-77), may have been short lived but was the blue touchpaper that inspired an explosion of new bands. This "New Wave", as well as leading to the formation of a hundred groups with a three chord repertoire, also threw up all manner of music ranging from the Industrial Death Factory music of Throbbing Gristle to the quirky sub pop of The Buzzcocks. More importantly, punk inspired a whole new attitude. A total rejection of society including the established musical landscape; bands like Pink Floyd, Yes and Genesis became boring old farts overnight. (Although, ironically, they are still breaking wind today). Rock was no longer perceived as elitist; everybody could take part, form a band, write a fanzine, even put out a record or start your own label. It was a whole new ball game.

At first, the English music press had attempted to ignore this new phenomenon clinging dearly to the established musical order. Slowly, however, resistance crumbled and publications like *Sounds* and the *New Musical Express*, began to cover this new explosion until its energy and diversity dominated their pages. The other two English weeklies of the time, *Melody Maker* and *Record Mirror,* also rather grudgingly covered the new music but in a much more half-hearted way.

As a result, a new generation of journalists emerged. They listened with their ears and guts rather than critical faculties. More importantly, they were more open-minded and positively went out of their way to hear the new bands that were crawling out of the woodwork. Always on the look out for the next big thing or something different to bring to the attention and turntables of their growing, eager readership. It was a time for new talent to flourish and justifiable proselytizing hype.

The Residents were eventually caught up in this. True, they were not a "New Wave" band (then again neither were Dire Straits, The Stranglers or The Police) but after four years of trading in obscurity they were grateful for an opportunity to market and sell their particular sound. The first article about The Residents in the English rock press was penned by Jon Savage. He read an article about them in the short lived, punk inspired, San Francisco-based fanzine *Search and Destroy*. Intrigued, he found out more about the band and included them in a *Sounds* survey of "New Musick" (26th November, 1977) along with Brian Eno, Devo, Throbbing Gristle and Kraftwerk. He described the music thus:

> "Mixture surprisingly attractive. Afterwards, most rock 'n' roll ridiculously 1D (dimensional) 2D straightforward. Vague air of undefinable menace, deeper subversion."[3]

A month later he enthusiastically reviewed *Meet The Residents, Third Reich and Roll* and *Fingerprince.*

> "What they offer is so radically different that effort is needed to break out of your/my box before you/I can fully enjoy... There is a deep design behind The Residents' sound: what they want they do know. But they're not telling. And why should they? This leaves room for your free-association, using Residents records as soundtrack. Often they are like waking dreams. Elements rearranged (deliberately) in such a way as to strike at the subconsciousness. Yes – that powerful. Think I'm trying to say that they're like nothing you/I have heard before."[4]

The exposure heralded a breakthrough. The Cryptic Corporation were so grateful for Savage's five star endorsement of their releases (***** equated with Very Important Platter) that that they sent him a telegram with five stars on it. Even better was to follow, Andy Gill, writing for the rival *New Musical Express*, began to add his enthusiastic endorsement. Suddenly they had two partisans in the very heart of the two most influential British music magazines of the day.

There was also the important patronage of John Peel. Peel was, at the time, without doubt the most influential DJ on the air in England. Like The Residents themselves he was weaned on The Beatles and progressive music. However, he was open-minded enough to allow his ears to dictate what he played. Despite initial reservations he had fallen under the spell of punk and the New Wave and turned his nightly 10pm-12pm nationwide programme over to that type of music (with a nice slice of Reggae thrown in for good measure). At the time he was the only DJ who played "new wave" music on a regular basis. More importantly he did not simply play releases by the established new stars. He personally took great trouble to listen to anything and everything sent to him, from bedroom demo tapes to newly pressed singles on obscure one-shot labels. He was a music freak. If he liked something he played it. Simple as that.

Sent copies of various releases through a source at Virgin records, Peel found The Residents' music "Fresh, innovative and exciting", and began playing their records. His large devoted audience took note.

One of those "turned onto" The Residents in this manner was the illustrator Edwin Pouncey aka Savage Pencil. He recalls hearing "Flying" from *The Beatles Play The Residents and The Residents play The Beatles*. "I thought what the Hell is *this*?" He resolved to find out. It was hard work. No-one seemed to stock the record or know how to get hold of it. Finally he got in touch with Ralph Records and began buying the records direct. He "loved the music but also important were the graphics and artwork... I thought they were real artistic statements."[5]

More importantly, he had a weekly strip in *Sounds* called "Rock and Roll Zoo" – a satirical animalistic view of the music business – and did one on The Residents. This was so appreciated by Cryptic publicist Jay Clem, that Pouncey was told that he would never have to buy a Residents' record again. Pouncey also did a "Santa Dog" collage which he sent to them which was eventually given away in limited edition to members of WEIRD; The Residents first fan club (1978-81).

Another notable convert was Chris Cutler, drummer in the seminal, Jazz rock improvisation and no compromise band, Henry Cow. He got to hear of The Residents via Jumbo Van Rennen who performed A&R duties for Virgin – Henry Cow's record company. Van Rennen said that the music was great, but that Virgin would never touch them. (In fact, Virgin America later made an offer which the Cryptic Corporation rejected). Cutler took the records, listened to them and found some kindred spirits. He started to correspond with the band. More importantly as Henry Cow were in the process of splitting up, he was starting up his own company with his partner Nick Hobbs – Recommended Records – to distribute the music of bands he found particularly interesting, but who were totally unknown outside of a devoted but limited circle. He offered to distribute Ralph Records in England and Europe. Chris Cutler:

> "We were the first people to bring the records in and we held onto our monopoly effectively when other people started to bring them in. So, for a very long time we were the main distributor."[6]

Therefore under this agreement Residents records began appearing in English shops. As imports they were slightly more expensive than other records, but most importantly people who had heard and liked this weird sounding American band or read about them in the music press could finally go out and buy their records.

In 444 Grove Street this sudden attention saw a hive of activity most notably in the mail order department. Whereas previously the Cryptic Corporation had literally not been able to give the records away, they were now inundated with orders. Demand even began to outstrip supply. The initial 1,000 copies of *Third Reich and Roll* and *Fingerprince* had sold out by December 1977 – "Due to a delightfully surprising increase in demand the album is temporarily out of stock" – The Cryptic Corporation were not slow in re-pressing or issuing new product.

Although The Residents were reported to have been stuck inside the musical igloo of their latest "concept" album, *Eskimo*, for the last two years, this did not stop them swiftly recording and releasing the *Duck Stab* EP in February 1978. Knowing that there was a market for the product, The Cryptic Corporation initially produced 2,500 copies – and when they began to sell like hot cakes, they pressed a further 12,500!

Duck Stab was a seminal Residents record. It was more than favourably reviewed – "dazzling breadth and diversity,"[7] – winning further converts due to its quirky accessibility. Each of the seven tracks were distinctly Residential but were each imbued with the catchiness of nursery rhymes. The breathless run of "Constantinople", the tongue-in-cheek pastiche of the "Booker Tease", almost ballad-like "Blue Rosebuds" sliced open at intervals with a falsetto knife, the squeaky "Bach Is Dead", the humorous "Elvis And His Boss", the ho-ho-ho "Laughing Song" and the surreal "Sinister Exaggerator" are all of normal song length but typical Residential construction. Snakefinger's guitar work is simply the icing on the cake.

The packaging was again superb and artistically stood out from the cut and paste of the New Wave herd. The surrealist black and red cover of a man stabbing a duck commanded attention. For the first time the lyrics were printed on the back sleeve. With an eye to the collectors' market there was also a limited edition package of *Duck Stab* T-shirt, single and colour poster. The only blemish was the appalling sound quality due, in part, to the fact that there was over 16 minutes of music crammed onto the two sides of the EP. Later that year *Duck Stab* was re-released with another batch of songs that were supposed to have become a second EP. This LP became known as *Duck Stab/Buster and Glen*. The music on the *Buster and Glen* side was every bit as good and accessible as the *Duck Stab* songs and the album sold strongly.

More significantly, hot on the heels of *Duck Stab* came the re-release of "Satisfaction". The Residents had been keen to keep the original version as a limited edition "art" piece and not re-release it in any form. However, such was the demand, they finally bowed to commercial forces and allowed its reissue. They would have been foolhardy not to. Although not typical of their output, the screamed vocals and manic delivery of the song fitted perfectly into the punk rock/new wave musical bag. It was hard fast music, painful to listen to and totally irreverent to The Rolling Stones' original. Its ferocity matched anything being produced by punk rock's market leaders.

However, concept band Devo's cover version of "Satisfaction" was released in England two weeks before The Residents re-released theirs. Whereas The Residents overloaded the song, Devo stripped it down. It too worked very well. As for what the

Cryptic's thought about it: "The Residents had Devo's version beat by two years, why should those spuds get all the money now?!"[8]

Despite the competition, the re-released "Satisfaction" found an eager audience. Some 30,000 copies were printed on translucent yellow vinyl and began flying out in England, Europe and America. It became, at that time, the biggest selling Residents' record netting the band some $20,000.

Flushed with growing success, Ralph Records also released the first solo single by long time collaborator Snakefinger. Not that he had planned to record it. J.Raul Brody:

"He was working on a pop demo tape because he really wanted to score a major label deal and so came to The Residents studio... and his deal with The Residents was, in exchange for them letting him use the studio and their production time to make these quirky little pop demos – which, I believe turned The Residents' stomachs – Phillip would agree to work with them on a Residents sounding song. That was "The Spot"."[9]

Released on blue vinyl this song about paranoia launched Snakefinger's long and productive solo career on Ralph Records.

Unlike other American bands like Talking Heads, Blondie, Devo and Pere Ubu that were breaking in England at the time, The Residents could not follow up this media attention with a series of live concerts to promote either themselves or their new releases. Publicist Jay Clem had been quick to make himself available for interview and propagation of The Residents' music and the mythos surrounding the band. The Theory of Phonetic Organisation, the mysterious N. Senada, the lengths to which The Residents went to keep their identities secret and their abandoned feature film *Vileness Fats* were all trotted out time after time like a team of highly trained circus horses. However, even the fact that The

Residents sounded and acted unlike any other band on earth was unlikely to generate anything other than an occasional feature as a supplement to record reviews. Photographs even began to appear that purported to reveal who The Residents really were (Flynn and Kennedy at a Pere Ubu concert, the Chinese Gang of Four...) As 1978 wound to a close something else was required to keep The Residents in the public eye. Then, an idea came about.

"We no longer have The Residents. They're missing." So said Jay Clem to Michael Goldberg of the *Berkeley Barb* on 8th September, 1978.

The day before they were due to deliver the completed *Eskimo* tapes to The Cryptic Corporation, The Residents vanished in a puff of smoke and re-appeared in London with Chris Cutler. They left the *Eskimo* tapes with him and then flew off en-masse to Japan. "...they weren't pleased with some of our marketing techniques"; Jay Clem related to the *New Musical Express*, "they felt we were promoting them too fast, and endangering the anonymity that they feel is vital to their creative process."[10]

The Cryptic Corporation's response to this was to release "some old tapes they left lying around the studio."[11] Which was, rather conveniently, the *Not Available* album. (In fact they were on the master shelf and clearly marked). A full page advert was placed in the English music press on 4th November 1978 – "Now it can be sold" - and the following week Jay Clem and John Kennedy arrived in London to retrieve the missing master tapes. They also used the time to hold fruitful negotiations with various record companies who had expressed an interest in signing The Residents or licensing their records for release. The *Eskimo* tapes were handed back to a snazzily dressed John Kennedy by Chris Cutler outside the National Safe Deposit Box Company in the City of London where they had been stored. The whole "event" was of course photographed and reported by attendant journalists. The icing on the cake of this happy ending was the reappearance of The Residents in San Francisco.

It was, a marketing scam. Pure and simple. And it worked. As Chris Cutler states, "the media paid a lot of attention to it. Made them come and take photographs.."[12] In addition it not only increased interest in the unfinished *Eskimo* but gave The Cryptic Corporation good cause to finally release *Not Available* onto a market eager for new Residents' product. As for The Residents they just got on with playing with their new sixteen track studio installed under the watchful eyes of Hardy Fox and Homer Flynn. They celebrated by whacking out another version of "Fire" from the original 1972 *Santa Dog*. It was given away free as a Christmas card with the original version on the flipside to everybody on Ralph Records mailing list, along with an "official" explanation as to why The Residents had disappeared.

As for *Not Available*, – "according to the theory of obscurity, the LP cannot be released until its makers literally forget it exists"[13] – we are led to believe that this was The Residents' second LP recorded in 1974. If so, the difference between this and *Meet The Residents* is astounding. Not only in sound quality – there is much more space in the mix – but in compositional strength. *Meet The Residents* was very rudimentary music. Roughly recorded and roughly played. *Not Available* is much more assured, both in execution and studio technique. Although it was alleged to have been recorded in 1974 there was probably some fine tuning and perhaps even some re-recording done in the four years before release. Whatever, it was definitely recorded on an eight track machine.

Not Available is a surreal opera divided into four suites, the music is haunting, darkly compelling. The "plot" is literally unfathomable, as much of the poetic lyricism is elusive and somewhat unintelligable due to extensive vocal multi-tracking. However, combined with the music it has a strong powerful effect. Synthesiser and piano carries the recurring thematic motif. All The Residents' trademarks are in evidence – multi-tracked horns, vocals dredged groaning, screaming, mewing, whining and full of spell-like invocation out of a Louisiana swamp, quirky rhythms, piano and a host of studio trickery. Conceptually, one might be tempted to compare *Not Available* to something like *Dark Side of The Moon* by Pink Floyd but this would be misleading. For all of its groundbreaking innovation *Dark Side of The Moon* is still a collection of "rock" songs, albeit innovatively arranged and recorded. *Not Available* is all concept and sound. There are no specific "songs" only semi-operatic suites that Andy Gill was correct in describing as "...some of the most haunting music The Residents have ever produced..,"[14] More importantly, after the sheer dissonance of "Satisfaction" and the quirky accessibility of *Duck Stab/Buster and Glen*, The Residents had revealed, in the space of twelve months, the breadth of their studio-based musical explorations. Their restless refusal to settle into one particular musical niche.

Eskimo would confirm this.

Footnotes
1. Jon Savage, *Sounds*, 31st December 1977
2. Andy Gill, *New Musical Express*, 13th May 1978
3. Jon Savage, *Sounds*, November 26th, 1877.
4. Jon Savage, *Sounds*, 31st December 1977.
5. Edwin Pouncey. Interview with the Author, January 1993.
6. Chris Cutler. Interview with the Author, August 1992.
7. Jon Savage. *Sounds* 4th February 1978.
8. Cryptic *Book of The Residents*, 1986.
9. J Raul Brody. Interview with Author October 1992.

10. Interview with Jay Clem by Andy Gill. *New Musical Express*, 11th November
    1978.
11. *Berkeley Barb* , 8th September 1978.
12. Chris Cutler. Interview with Author. August 1992.
13. Sleevenotes from *Third Reich and Roll*.
14. Andy Gill, *New Musical Express*. 11th November 1978.

ESKIMO

FUTURE: let me back up for a moment. You mentioned N. Senada, and I'm aware that he is often mentioned as a major influence.

RESIDENT#4: If you wanted to get right down to it, all that we are, we owe to him. He is possibly the last remaining unique individual. Our entire musical concept stems directly from his Bavarian works.

RESIDENT#3: With a fear of being premature, I'll venture to comment that we received a cassette from N. about a year ago which he recorded at the North Pole with the Eskimos. We have been reinterpreting this tape for our 5th album. It is perhaps the hardest thing we've attempted yet, (to other Residents)... Y'all think it's OK to say that, don't you? (Others shrug their shoulders).

RESIDENT#2: You see, the thing is that the album is so unique in its structure, that we are hesitant to discuss it until it is further along.

FUTURE: And when is that to be?

RESIDENTS: (all laugh) Eskeymow! Eskeymow! Eskeymow![1]

The one truth that lay behind the *Eskimo* tapes publicity scam was that *Eskimo* was not finished. Like *Vileness Fats* it was an ambitious, mammoth undertaking and even The Residents themselves were unsure if they could complete it. Hardy Fox:

> "Music had to be written that was reasonably true to Eskimo life. It had to be written using a limited scale and with a very simplistic, primitive sound. So the music was being recorded just on its own, and simultaneously sound effects were being collected for the stories, and gradually the whole thing was being assembled.
>
> It was started on an 8-track but it was discovered that it was impossible to do on an 8-track. The mixing was incredible even on a 16-track, because everything was squeezed in so tightly that there was just no space between one thing and another. Something was always going out and something else coming in because they had to share tracks. All the way through it was like a giant puzzle. And there was very much a concern that it might not make a very interesting record, because there was just no way of telling until it was finished."[2]

Why they had embarked upon such an ambitiously esoteric project in the first place – an attempt to document Eskimo life and culture on record – was due to an alleged reestablishment of contact with the mysterious N. Senada. He had conveniently spent most of his time since 1972 studying Eskimo culture and had sent tapes of his research to The Residents. He even allegedly turned up at the studio, "In the middle of the night with a thermos flask full of Arctic air. He was very excited. "Get this on tape" he kept saying. He thought we should all live in a refrigerator for a year"[3], a Resident explained.

The real reason for this attempt at an aural cultural documentary was probably more to do with The Residents' fascination with sound and musical restlessness than slavish devotion to a possibly mythical guru. Throughout their career The Residents had shown that they had no interest in simply regurgitating what they had already done. Their music was only limited by the endless possibilities of studio technique. *Eskimo* was an attempt to take the concept of studio recording further than it had ever been taken before. To create an aural documentary.

The long drawn out recording of *Eskimo* featured the usual quota of other musicians. Every Residents' project from *Meet The Residents* onwards had featured the talents of additional players. So, despite the marketing ploy of remaining anonymous they were also becoming highly collaborative. Or as a Cryptic spokesman put it:

> "The Residents are record producers; if they have to play instruments to get something across, if they have to hire studio musicians, they do."[4]

For *Eskimo*, as well as Snakefinger, they used Don Preston – (ex keyboard player with Frank Zappa's Mothers of Invention who had been introduced to The Residents by Jazz composer Carla Bley) and Chris Cutler who, after extensive correspondence, had flown out to meet and record with them in April 1978:

> "It was with interest therefore and a certain excitement that I approached the windowless warehouse on 444 Grove Street where the Cryptic Corporation have their offices... Here I found a genuine recording company with studios, conference rooms, a graphics studio, photographic darkrooms, shipping and receiving offices and, still under construction, filming and live performance facilities."[5]

As for his contribution to the *Eskimo* project:

> "There were finished pieces, half-finished pieces and blank tape and I played along with some stuff that was half-finished, almost finished... I put stuff on tape for them to use as they wanted later... It was professional, straight ahead, fairly creative and inventive, but a lot of studio work is."[6]

Working with these allegedly mysterious musicians was apparently no big deal. There was no curtain in the studio, no disguises or darkened rooms. Sometimes all of The Residents would be there, sometimes he might be working with only one or two of them; "On a musical level, as far as I could see, there were really two..."

Cutler gained an insight into the way The Residents worked at the time:

> "They would clock in every day just like going to work. Nine o'clock in the morning. Get there, open the doors, look at the mail, have a cup of coffee and discuss what they were going to do for the day. Work on their various projects. Five, half past five, go home. Every day. If you want to be romantic, it was like Andy Warhol's factory. If you want to be unromantic it was like a day job. A bit of a weird day job, but the product they were producing was a weird product."[7]

Eskimo was finally unleashed onto the world in October 1979. It sold more copies in the first five weeks than every other previous Ralph release combined. Everything about the record was perfect. The packaging was superb. The first 10,000 copies were pressed on "Arctic white" vinyl. The sleeve itself was a gatefold with the various Eskimo stories to be read in conjunction with the music inside. The most striking aspect of the packaging was the front cover. The Residents stood decked out in top hats, tails, white dress shirts, bow ties and canes against an Arctic background. Four huge head-sized eyeballs disguised their features. The effect of this image was quite stunning and became an instant trademark and eventual albatross.

Interestingly enough, the eyeballs were not going to be featured at all. Homer Flynn, the Cryptic Officer responsible for (porno) graphic design recalls initially wanting to have silver heads reflecting Arctic mist, only abandoning the idea after discovering they were virtually impossible to manufacture to his specifications. The eyeballs were his second choice. Fortunately, they were very easy to manufacture, and relatively cheap at a total cost of $1,800, and were fabricated by a company called Dinosaur products that specialised in theatrical props and effects for feature films.

As for the music, it met with critical acclaim. Andy Gill in the *New Musical Express*:

> "It's without doubt one of the most important albums ever made, if not *the* most important. Quite simply, The Residents are halfway up the ladder while the rest are still trying to find a place to put it so it won't fall over when they step onto the bottom rung."[8]

Eskimo is in many respects one of the jewels in the Residential crown. It went on to sell over 100,000 copies worldwide, a fantastic amount for an independent record, especially considering the musical content. *Eskimo* was hardly easy listening. It was an aural documentary, "a moody collection of abstract melodies, punctuated by primitive vocals and rhythms which tells the legends of the Eskimo people entirely through the use of sound."[9] Each part glides into the other from the opening melody of "The Walrus Hunt", to "Birth", "Arctic Hysteria", "The Angry Angakok", "A Spirit Steals a Child" to the final "Festival Of Death". Musically it is typically Residential with an emphasis upon collectiveness and studio technique. The efforts that must have gone into creating this musical opus were considerable. The Residents read voraciously, built their own Eskimo ceremonial instruments and spent a great deal of time working out the phonetics of the language. Hardy Fox:

> "Most of the lyrics are English words that approximate the sound of an actual Eskimo word. That's the only thing that was really

worked with. You'll have a whole series of English words that when strung together sound vaguely like Eskimo. Authentic Eskimo, at that."[10]

Some of these chanted "English words" were recognisable as TV advertisement slogans of the time. "You deserve a break today," "Coca Cola adds life", and, "We are Driven!" leading some cynics to suggest that the entire record was simply another Residential practical joke rather than a serious work of art. This was something Hardy Fox strenuously denied:

> "One of the things I want to clarify is that some of the people who have noticed that, have started assuming that that's what the lyrics are throughout the record. That's not the case. It's only in the one section, and it relates to the fact that at that point in the story, the Eskimos are being subjected more and more to Western civilization and culture. As a result, their native chants start changing into commercial slogans."[11]

Eskimo had been a long arduous job of work, but to show that they did not take themselves that seriously, in April of the following year The Residents released a disco version of *Eskimo* called *Diskomo*. The entire LP was condensed into eight minutes and propelled by a disco beat. The other side of this 12" single – "Goosebump" – was a number of songs played on children's instruments raided from a local Toys R Us and treated with adult effects like reverb, echo, multi-tracking etc. Basically, The Residents were having a little fun at their own expense.

And why not? At this time they were America's most successful independent band. They even had their own devoted fan club formed in June 1978. The aptly named W.E.I.R.D. (We Endorse Immediate Resident Deification) was formed by Resident devotees Phil Culp and Mimi King. The Residents remained aloof although the Cryptic Corporation did allow distinctive applications – "Ignorance of your culture is not considered cool" – to be placed inside LP cover sleeves to attract membership.

Culp and King had an overwhelming response and they soon had over 500 replies and membership fees. The membership package took a long time to appear but when it did it was superb; not only was there the typical "membership card" but also *The Official W.E.I.R.D. Book of The Residents*, an excellent, if somewhat mythical history of the band. It was written by music journalist and Residents' fan Matt Groening who later went on to create The Simpsons. Cover art was by Gary Panter.

W.E.I.R.D only lasted for three years, 1978-1981, with membership peaking at over a thousand. It experienced tremendous administrative problems although it did deliver what it promised – limited edition fine art prints by artists Gary Panter and Savage Pencil, snips of the *Eskimo* master tape and the occasional newsletter – usually several months late. It finally closed down in 1981 after releasing the "Babyfingers" single. The missing side of the *Fingerprince* LP. Full cover art by Poreknowgraphics.

Footnotes
1. Interview with *Future* fanzine. No 2. (New York 1977).
2. Hardy Fox, *Keyboard*, October 1982.
3. A Resident to Chris Cutler. *Sounds*, 13th May 1978.
4. A Cryptic spokesman to *Bam*, 1st September 1978.
5. Chris Cutler, *Sounds* 13th May 1978.
6. Chris Cutler, interview with Author. August 1992.
7. Chris Cutler, interview with Author. August 1992.
8. Andy Gill. *New Musical Express* 8th October 1979.
9. *Cryptic Book of The Residents*. (1986).
10. Hardy Fox, *Keyboard*. October 1982.
11. Ibid.

Who the hell are The Residents...? 4

Cartoon by Savage Pencil from Rock and Roll Zoo

RALPH RECORDS – BUY OR DIE!

"This is not a rule or anything, but it turns out that every artist on our label had material out on an album before we signed them. For one thing, this gives us something to listen to, and it also shows us that here is a group of people who have a reasonably realistic view about things. When you talk to a guy who has done his own record, you don't have to be talking hundreds of thousands of dollars, because that guy knows what it takes. He knows how it can be done cheaply, and he's not afraid to do it cheaply and make certain sacrifices to get things done.

There is no way in hell that we can compete with any major or quasi-major record company when it comes to dollars and cents, in terms of signing a band. But we do have the built-in advantage that we don't have to compete with them, because the type of people we are interested in are generally not of much interest to the majors anyway."[1]

Jay Clem

Eskimo marked the high watermark of interest in The Residents. It became their best selling record to date and even charted in Greece! However, with an eye to the future there was another significant release at this time.

Subterranean Modern released a month after *Eskimo* was Ralph Records first tentative foray into releasing music by other artists. (Snakefinger and Schwump had been friends). The album was a "sampler" that featured the cream of San Francisco's avant-garde scene. Chrome, Tuxedomoon and MX80 Sound were all given one fourth of an LP and artistic licence to record whatever they pleased. The only ground rule laid down was that each had to contribute a "version" of Tony Bennett's classic potboiler "I Left My Heart in San Francisco."

Chrome, led by Damon Edge and Helios Creed were established studio explorers who had already released three LP's on their own Siren label. The first, *The Visitation* (1976), was Hendrix influenced, but with *Alien Soundtracks* and *Half Machine Lip Moves,* they metamorphasised their four track world into a collision of rock, sci-fi lyricism and very Dadaist cut-up tape techniques to produce some very effective, original and disturbing music. They had never performed live. "They're not ready for us"[2], sneered Edge who spent most of his time prowling around in a lab coat and Velvet Underground shades.

Tuxedomoon, on the other hand, were frequent live performers on the local San Francisco scene. Formed in 1977, conceptually they were closely related to The Residents in the way that they sought to combine art, music, theatre and film. Their music was moody, textural and explorative. Avant-rock blended with classical motifs and electronics.

Alongside these two excellent and very distinctive groups, MX-80 Sound were something of an oddity. Turgid sub-metal rhythms that sound as if their portion of *Subterranean Modern* had been some kind of pressing error. It was neither innovative, experimental or in any way avant-garde.

As for The Residents, they contributed three excellent tracks especially recorded for the project and the best "reading" of "I Left My Heart" (Chrome hissed out some white noise, Tuxedomoon contributed a telephone call for Welfare whilst the melody was buzzed out on harmonica in the background. As for MX-80 Sound they gave it, surprise, surprise, a rather, uh, heavy instrumental reading). On the whole, *Subterranean Modern* with its fantastic Gary Panter cover art (the first sleeve not done by Pornographics), was (or at least three parts of it) "light-years ahead of any comparable compilation release this year."[3]

Of the three bands Tuxedomoon and MX-80 were signed to Ralph Records. Chrome too were offered a deal but they haggled so much that Ralph eventually withdrew their offer. They eventually signed with Beggars Banquet in England.

At the time it was felt that MX-80 Sound had commercial potential. In 1977 when based in Bloomington, Indiana they had sent a demo tape to Island Records in England at a time when record companies were signing anything that was hard and fast. The demo was released as *Hard Attack* and it sold over 25,000 copies on the back of rabid reviews – "The Bloomington Sound – the next big thing?"[4] However, unable to promote the LP in Europe with a tour – they all had day jobs – the arrival of the real new wave left them high and dry. Island dropped them and they relocated to San Francisco and eventually fell into the arms of Ralph Records.

The Cryptic Corporation's reasoning behind expansion was sound. By building a label of like-minded artists they could widen the appeal of Ralph Records. They hoped that the interest generated by The Residents would rub off upon their labelmates. They no longer courted major label acceptance, they changed tack and attempted to turn Ralph Records into a large flourishing successful independent label. As Jay Clem explained:

"For one thing, we have a lot of facilities right here in the building. We have a complete graphics facility for doing our own album covers. We have our own recording studio. When you have your own studio, you don't have to go out and pay $50,000 or something to rent one. Another thing is that we don't spend a lot of frill money the way other record companies do. We can't. We just don't have it. The people who work here work in large part as a labour of love. Nobody is paid a fair market value for their services.

We also do our own distribution. We do use other distributors as well, but we are the distributor to the distributors, as opposed to sending the master to someone in a licensing deal. Doing that we would cut our profits down to half, if not a third or a fourth. We service some stores directly. And on the retail level we had our own mail-order operation, so we also get some of the retailer profits. Even though the volumes are all very low, it adds up to enough that we are allowed to continue. We have found that in spite of what everybody in the world will tell you, you can make an album for a decent amount of money."[5]

With expansion, The Cryptic Corporation found themselves taking on additional staff. The first through the door was Tom Timony. He got to hear of the job through Clem's girlfriend and she put his name forward. He was interviewed by Clem.

"Everybody else, sort of peered down – there was this balcony - looking at me. I guess they gave their nod of approval. I was hired."[6] At first, the working relationship was tentative. After all, the Cryptics/Residents were all long time friends and "...for years were an in-house co-op. There was never any outside world connection. I was someone they let in."[7] Initially, Timony was a general factotum, answering the telephone, packing mail order items – essentially "Jay Clem's whipping boy" and other sundry tasks. He also had to suffer their varied musical tastes; African tribal percussion, Indonesian Gamelan, film scores and Ennio

Morriocone he could take, however, "One of The Residents loved Led Zeppelin. They used to drive me crazy playing Led Zeppelin albums..."[8] Timony gives a bird's eye view of what it was like at this time.

> "When I came in it was a free for all. Lots of money being spent, lots of product being made, just way out of proportion. There was the big independent scene... The Residents were in the right place at the right time to be caught up in that. It was like a playland of we'll write all these cheques. They signed MX-80, Tuxedomoon. They were riding on a lot of the money The Residents were making, people put money into the company. I came into the company as a non-business person and thought what the Hell are these people doing?"[9]

The Cryptic Corporation did not just sign bands, they also gave them advances in the region of $10,000 - $20,000. Jay Clem was concerned with being scrupulously fair. So much so that the contracts he drew up ran to fifty pages and covered such esoteric areas as the division of royalties from sales on American army bases. When Tuxedomoon could not afford to pay a lawyer to read through their contract, Clem arranged for Ralph Records to lend the band the money to hire one. This lawyer then proceeded to advise his clients to seek more favourable terms from Ralph who were meeting his fees.

There was also a heavy investment in promotion. One innovative idea was an ongoing series of *Buy Or Die* 7" EP singles. These were, in effect, miniature *Subterranean Modern*s featuring four tracks from four artists taken from their latest Ralph releases. In effect, an aural edition of the previous mail order *Buy Or Die* catalogues. They were offered in a large advertising campaign restricted to the United States and Canada – *Billboard, Rolling*

Stone etc – for the token price of $1.00 which included postage and packaging. Even though Ralph Records would be losing money on each of the singles sold, it was hoped that in the long term they would recoup on their investment by people liking what they heard and subsequently purchasing an album or albums by Ralph artists.

The first *Buy Or Die* featured excerpts from the current LP releases by Snakefinger, MX-80 Sound, Tuxedomoon and The Residents. There were three *Buy Or Die* EP's in all, each corresponding to a relevant mail order catalogue. Around 12-15,000 of each EP were pressed. Sometimes hundreds would be mailed out in a single day. Artwork for all three was done by Gary Panter. In the long term they did work as a marketing tool, and the cost of producing them was recouped by mail order and direct sales.

A lot of established Residents' fans bought the albums and singles by these new Ralph acts on faith. The reasoning was simple; if it was on The Residents' label then they must like it, so it must be good. In many respects it was. Most of these early Ralph releases were excellent, from the aural soundscapes of Tuxedomoon, the eclectic guitar work of Fred Frith, to the sub techno wizardry of Yello. The Residents even produced and played on the first two Snakefinger albums.

Although Tuxedomoon and MX80-Sound came from the flourishing local San Francisco scene, other Ralph acts were signed in the traditional sense. The Residents had always received tapes. Demos, people whacking off on their instruments and even hamfisted attempts to cover Residents' material. As early as February 1978 they were asking that these tapes be restricted to "your most interesting selections" and that "editing is no sin."[10] It was through this medium that The Cryptic Corporation signed two experimental sound groups from Europe; Renaldo and the Loaf and Yello.

Renaldo and the Loaf were based in Portsmouth, England. Like The Residents, they were less of a band than two people interested in making tapes in the evenings and at weekends. Eventually in 1979 these self-produced noises made it onto their own privately released tape – *Renaldo and the Loaf Play Struve and Sneff.* Amongst other things, Renaldo and the Loaf were such rabid Residents' fans that they even wrote songs in response to The Residents fan club competition seeking meanings of W.E.I.R.D. – "Walk Energetically In Rubber Dungarees", "Watch Escapism It's Rather Daft", "Waste Eleven Iron Rubber Dummies" etc. etc. etc.

They also contributed tracks to *South Specific*, a "sampler" of local Portsmouth talent released in August 1980. This, however, was only the beginning. When Brian "Renaldo" Poole went on a fly-drive holiday to America with some friends:

"We stopped off in San Francisco for a couple of days and being into The Residents I was naturally curious to see where 444 Grove Street was and what it looked like. Found it. Just rang the doorbell and went in. Apparently – I was told retrospectively – that I was very, very lucky. It was only because I'd come all the way from England that I was allowed in. I dropped a copy of my tape in."[11]

Poole later found out that..

"..the person I'd actually handed the tape to at Grove Street happened to be a Resident who was at the Ralph HQ on that day. I understand it was The Residents' own request that we were brought onto Ralph. They liked what they heard."[12]

Subsequently, Jay Clem (armed with a 50 page contract) flew to England to sign the band. Renaldo and The Loaf produced additional material during 1980 that became *Songs for Swinging Larvae.*

It was a similar story with the Swiss electronic trio Yello. TV repairman Boris Blank and musical associate Carlos Peron dropped in a demo tape of songs and were told that if they could produce another with less hiss on it, Ralph would release it. This led to *Solid Pleasure* with its totally original rhythmic electronic soundscape and the distinctive vocals of globe trotting artiste Deiter Meier. So began the musical career of one of Switzerland's biggest exports since banking services and Swatches.

Tuxedomoon and Yello met with critical acclaim and even Renaldo and the Loaf's LP's made money for the parent company. But despite their growing success, Ralph Records were very conscious of the fact that they were operating, especially in America, outside the normal industry parameters with music that was in no way suited for the commercial mainstream. True, they had built up a solid relationship with the independent College radio station network across America. (The second Residents radio sampler *Please Do Not Steal It!* had initially been mailed to 850 stations in 1977). However, they wanted to explore as many avenues of promotion as possible. Therefore in addition to the *Buy Or Die* EPs they hit upon the idea of promotional films.

Given The Residents' early experiments in this medium it was an obvious avenue to explore. Apart from the abandoned *Vileness Fats,* in 1977 they had produced a fantastic 16mm promotional film to accompany *Third Reich and Roll* for an early innovative video programme in Australia called *Flashez.* Filmed between 1972-77 this short promo was described by Michael Shore in his *The Rolling Stone Book of Rock Video* as "the most utterly, exuberently original and bizarre performance video ever." I cannot better his description of "four maniacs in neo-Ku Klux Klan hoods and robes made out of newspapers, banging on trash cans and oil drums in a futuristic-tribal trash compactor mutilation of the sixties rock classic Land of 1,000 Dances."[13]

The Residents, who already owned lights, a 16mm camera and Grove Street, had ample warehouse space to use for indoor location shooting. However, rather than employing their own talents, The Residents entrusted long-time collaborator Graeme Whifler to produce these 'promos' for Ralph's new artists, as well as The Residents themselves.

Whifler set about his task with relish, and despite low budgets, developed a unique and arresting style, although not without problems. The original budget for the Renaldo and The Loaf video was $6,000 but it had to be totally re-shot after it was discovered that the footage was out of focus. This, and other production expenses eventually saw the video costing $21,000. More, incidentally, than it cost to record the LP. Whifler also made promotional films for Snakefinger's *Man in the Dark Sedan*, Tuxedomoon's notorious *Jinx*, and MX-80 Sound's aptly named *Why Are We Here?* As for The Residents, he was responsible for *Hello Skinny* and two of the *One Minute Movies*.

Whifler's technique was inspired by TV rather than cinematic imagery:

> "Even though we were working in film, I was well aware of the dynamic of the tube (TV), which could withstand wide angles, and I was, in several cases, intending to parody commercials while promoting the music... I never went for a lot of post-production, low budgets notwithstanding. If it's not on the film it's not there. You should do it all with the camera."[14]

Whifler's first piece for The Residents was *Hello Skinny*. Produced in 1980 it was intended to be the first in a series of short promotional films based around the user friendly *Duck Stab/Buster and Glen* album. The "Star" of this film was one Bridget Terris. As Homer Flynn relates:

> "Graeme brought this guy around about the time the film was happening and he was dressed in like, black gay leather drag... He had just been released from a mental institution. He had been put inside because he thought that he was Bridget Bardot. Everybody called him Bridget."[15]

However, Bridget was perfect for the part; he was, as the song required, "incredibly thin". However, before filming was completed he decided to leave San Francisco and catch a bus home. Therefore Whifler crafted the promotional film out of a series of black and white photographic stills of Bridget along with Resident eyeball montages and brief snippets of completed colour live actio. footage. The finished product with its dark, compelling, almost freak show visuals, was a perfect accompaniment to the eerie throbbing music.

Produced a year before the innovative but conservative AOR-minded MTV hit the airwaves, promotional films like *Hello Skinny* mainly received exposure in art houses, campuses and festivals in America, as well as limited exposure on European TV. However, there was critical acclaim heaped upon Whifler's work – "There's a very distinctive personality, a point of view to Whifler's mastery of camera work and color schemes and lighting".[16] The lack of outlets for these fledgling video productions, and initially poor sales for some of these new artists, slowly saw the opportunities to direct more promotional films dry up. However, in an attempt to retain his brilliant visual sense, later The Residents offered him $1,500 a month (the same amount they were paying themsleves at this time) to direct the Mole Show project. As he had never directed a live show, Whifler was uncomfortable with the idea, especially as The Residents already had a good idea of what they wanted in mind. There was an amicable parting and Whifler moved to LA. After working on a few other "Pop" promos for Sparks and Translator he vanished from sight, but has recently emerged as a co-credited screenwriter on the horror film *Doctor Giggles* (1992).

Whether Whifler's films actually encouraged sales is a moot point, in some respects they were ahead of their time as promotional film/video was in its infancy and the forum for showing "independent" work virtually non-existent. However, the films were innovative, visually compelling and "everything to do with advancing a fledgling art form." More importantly as Homer Flynn stated "The Ralph videos were definitely in line with our aesthetic."[17]

Footnotes
1. Jay Clem to *Keyboard* magazine, October 1982.
2. *New Musical Express*, 17th November 1979.
3. Andy Gill. *New Musical Express*, 5th January 1980
4. Chas De Whalley. *New Musical Express*, 31st December 1977.
5. Jay Clem to *Keyboard* magazine, October 1982.
6. Tom Timony. Interview with Author. October 1992.
7. Ibid.
8. Ibid.
9. Ibid.
10. Ralph Records mail order catalog. No. 3.
11. Brian Poole. Interview with Author. September 1992.
12. Ibid.
13. *Rolling Stones Book Of Rock Video* Michael Shore (Sidgwick & Jackson 1985). Page 65.
14. Graeme Whifler, *Record* magazine. October 1985.
15. Homer Flynn speaking at The Museum of Modern Art. October 19th 1992.
16. *Record* magazine, October 1986.
17. Homer Flynn, speaking at The Museum of Modern Art. October 19th 1992.

THE COMMERCIAL ALBUM

"...they approach recording the way an artist does a painting. They sit down with a blank canvas and start adding color. The things that aren't done right they paint over and paint something else back on top. This is still largely their approach to making a record."[1]

Jay Clem

"The thing that attracted me to The Residents work is that, unlike Laurie Anderson who will take something like a pitch shifter and stand there and speak into it, The Residents never pandered to the fascination the public has for the way it works. They use the technology to fulfill their artistic visions. They were not just going for cheap effects they were really looking at the effects and see how they could use them to fulfill a bigger picture."[2]

J. Raul Brody

Whilst this expansion was taking place The Residents themselves had not been idle. Indeed, they were positively attempting to sell themselves musically to the mainstream, albeit on their own terms. The way they decided to do this was by recording *The Commercial Album*, an LP of 40 one-minute songs. There was a plenitude of material... "*Eskimo* had been a very dominating project for a long time, and it didn't allow an outlet for a lot of things that were being written. There were piles of things, so the *Commercial Album* was an efficient way of getting rid of them."[3]

Possibly inspired by avant-garde composer John Cage's 1958/9 composition lecture series *Indeterminacy* where a series of thirty or forty stories and anecdotes were read out each lasting exactly one minute, *The Commercial Album* was also intended to make, "a direct commentary on the superficiality of pop music by incorporating more substance in one minute than most pop songs do in three or four."[4]

Unlike *Eskimo, The Commercial Album* was put together in an intensive ten month period between September 1979 and July 1980. As for how the songs were kept down to one minute...

"Basically, each song was worked out without regard to its length. Then it was a matter of starting to edit it using a stopwatch. Sections would be knocked out, or bars, or individual beats, until finally a basic cue track was written that was as close to one minute long as possible. From there, further operations were done with tape recorder speed and things like that to make the length exact."[5]

As usual, there were a number of collaborators on this project. Andy Partridge of XTC contributed vocals to "Margaret Freeman" and Lene Lovich sung distinctively on "Picnic Boy". Chris Cutler and Fred Frith also featured heavily on many tracks. When they came into the studio The Residents simply told them to play what and where they wanted. Both simply, "added parts".

The *Commercial Album* was the first Residents record to be licenced overseas (the *Nibbles* compilation aside). Prior to this Ralph had exported orders to various distributors. However, the *Commercial Album* was licenced to labels in England, France, Germany, Australia and New Zealand. In England, the licencee, PRE records even released a eight track "Commercial single" of

Above: Monitoring the progress of filming *Vileness Fats*. (Graeme Whifler)

Below: *Third Reich and Roll* publicity shot. (Pour No Graffix)

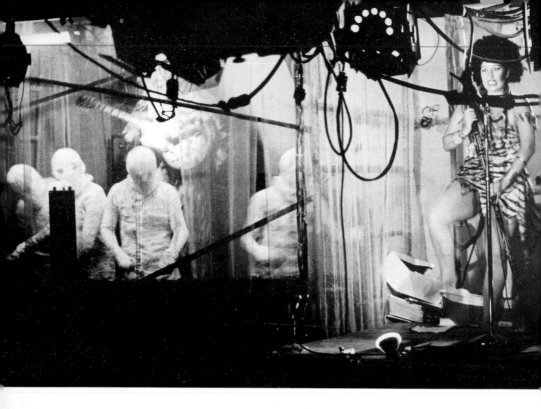

Above: Mummified live performance of "Six Things To A Cycle", Berkeley 1976.
(Richard McCaffree)

Below: The inside of The Residents' first studio in Sycamore Street.
(Pour No Graffix)

Above: The late Sun Ra, one of The Residents many and varied influences. (Harry Borden)

Opposite: Early on, the only press coverage The Residents could get was to dress in newspaper. (Pour No Graffix)

Below: From the photo shoot for the cover of Snakefinger's *Chewing Hides The Sound* LP. (Pour No Graffix)

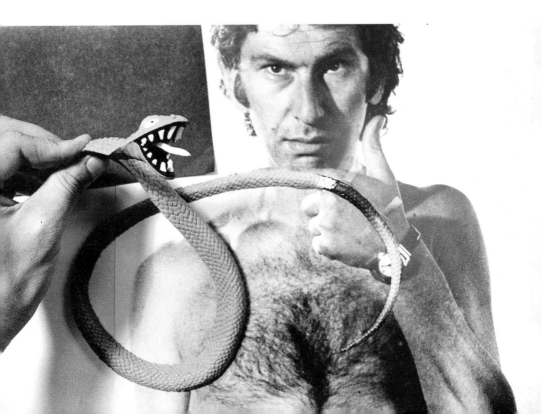

Top: The Residents resplendent in their tuxedo and eyeball combination posing for the cover of *Eskimo*. (Pour No Graffix)
Middle: The Residents take off their eyeballs for *Vacation* magazine whilst still cunningly concealing their identities. (Pour No Graffix)
Bottom: Chris Cutler handing the *Eskimo* master tapes back to John Kennedy. (Jay Clem)

Opposite: Three publicity photos; for *The Residents Play The Beatles*, at Niagara Falls and at Mount Rushmore. (Pour No Graffix)

The Residents performing The Mole Show.
(Randy Bachman)

Penn Jillette, narrator of The Mole Show.
(Pour No Graffix)

Jay Clem oversees Phillip "Snakefinger" Lithman
signing his contract with Ralph Records.
(Pour No Graffix)

A rather dazed looking Graeme Whifler.
(Pour No Graffix)

The Residents strutting their
"top hat and tails" stuff.
(Pour No Graffix)

Top left: The Residents lead singer performing on the 13th Anniversary tour.
(Rich Shupe)
Top right: The Residents and Snakefinger pose for a 13th Anniversary publicity
shot. (Pour No Graffix)
Bottom: The Residents in action on the 13th Anniversary tour. (Rich Shupe)

Top: The Residents posing with members of Jefferson Starship on an MTV promotional boat trip. (Pour No Graffix)

Middle: The Residents and dancers performing the Elvis segment to the Cube E show. (Henrik Kam)

Bottom: Publicity photo for the *Freak Show* LP. (Rex Ray and Jay Neel)

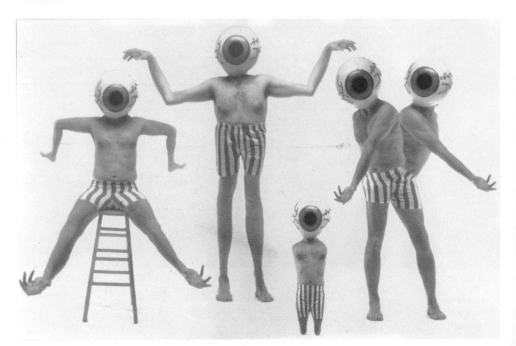

which two tracks – "Shut up Shut up" and "And I Was Alone" were unreleased tracks from the session.

The *Commercial Album* was heavily promoted in each country by the respective licencees and sold well. In San Francisco, The Cryptic Corporation used the novel marketing device of booking forty one-minute slots of advertising space on local radio station KFRC-AM and therefore by the end of the day had cunningly played the entire LP. There were also promotional films; *The One Minute Movies*.

These were financed by Phonogram and Celluoid records to promote the album in Europe. The generous budget allowed a great deal of work to go into them. "Moisture" and "The Simple Song" were directed by Graeme Whifler and "The Act of Being Polite" and "Perfect Love" by The Residents. *The Rolling Stone Book of Video* described them thus:

> "Petite pinnacles of haunting, dreamlike symbolism, each clip evoking serious otherworldly ritual... all four videos are stunning, because of The Residents incredible imagery and Whifler's equally awsome use of camera angles and movement, cutting and colour. Rock video doesn't come much better than this. Once seen the *One Minute Movies* cannot be forgotten."[6]

The pick of the bunch is "The Act of Being Polite", especially the image of the blonde-haired girl dressed all in red sitting down with a huge eyeball for a head grasping a package. "Simple Song" features The Residents' "strolling dance" in full tuxedo regalia around a roasting pig in the garden at the back of their Grove Street house. "Moisture" is full of autopsy/death symbolism and features a hilarious segment of a Resident energetically miming a guitar hero solo. "Perfect Love" – the weakest of all four – surreally suggests, in an *Eraserhead* manner – what can happen if you watch too much TV.

The *One Minute Movies* were eventually shown on MTV although they never received the "heavy rotation" they deserved.

Footnotes
1. Jay Clem to *Keyboard* magazine. October 1982.
2. J. Raul Brody.Interview with the Author.
3. Hardy Fox to *Keyboard* magazine. October 1982.
4. Jay Clem to *Vacation* Spring 1981.
5. Hardy Fox to *Keyboard* magazine.
6. *Rolling Stone Book Of Rock Video* (1985).

MOLE TOUR

"The Mole Show... is probably the worst business decision The Residents ever made, or at least the worst one we at the Cryptic Corporation allowed them to make."[1]

Homer Flynn

"Well, it was definitely a stone rolling through mud. Chaotic on a scale no-one was eager to repeat."[2]

Phil Perkins

One reason why The Residents had only played some three live shows in the ten years of their existence was less due to their reticence, than the fact that it was virtually impossible to recreate their multi-textural music in live performance. The handful of pre-Mole shows only served to demonstrate this fact. Their music was created in the studio for the sole purpose of being released on record. It was never intended for live performance.

However, with the advent of their popularity, The Residents began to contemplate touring, not only to promote themselves, but also to find out what it was like to actually play live over an extended period. Sail out into, what was for them, uncharted waters.

There had been tentative plans to take *Eskimo* out of the freezer and put it on the road in spectacular operatic style. The project never got off the ground, although they were playing "live" in their Grove Street studio as early as 1981. As Brian Poole recalls:

"I seem to have recollections of rehearsals going on for translating their music for potential live performance... rehearsing the songs we all know and love, to see how basically four people could perform them on stage. Whether the music which in itself was so much created in a studio context could be translated live. Various sorts of versions of things like "Birthday Boy" and "Hello Skinny". [3]

Nothing came of these rehearsals. Ironically, it was technology that came to their rescue. In 1981, a small company called EM-U Systems of California began marketing the Emulator onto an unsuspecting market. What EM-U had developed was the first musical technological advance since the introduction of synthesiser technology some 15 years previously.

The "Emulator" was one of the first samplers. Consisting of a small computer connected to a piano keyboard, it didn't generate any sound itself, but allowed the musician to record two seconds of sound through a microphone input and then replay this "sample" across each of the 12 tones and across four octaves.

The sound source could be anything. A dog barking, a handclap, two steel pipes banged together, a car exhaust, a voice, a trumpet, a guitar, a bass, a pre-recorded track. These sounds would be "replayed" perfectly. More importantly all of these "samples" could be stored on small computer floppy discs. Whenever they were required they could be slotted into the drive and "played." As a further refinement each "sample" could be speeded up or slowed down.

The groundbreaking versatility of this instrument was demonstrated to full effect in the film *Bladerunner*. The soundtrack composer Vangelis had used an Emulator to create parts of the soundtrack. The Residents were aware of this and one of them even went to see the film to specifically tape the original soundtrack in order to study the various unusual sounds produced by the Emulator. (Vangelis refused to sanction the release of the original score from *Bladerunner.*)

The Emulator was also an affordable item and The Residents soon acquired one. Being ardent technophiles, they ordered one as soon as they had read the promotional literature. They duly received one of the first machines off the production line – serial number #0005 – and locked themselves in the studio for six days only venturing out to grab anything in the Cryptic offices that they could "sample."

At first they saw this new toy as simply another compositional tool for their music. Indeed, they used it extensively on their next recording project, *The Tunes of Two Cities,* which officially became the first recording to feature an Emulator and "made really remarkable music that sounded like nothing else because they were drawing from a pallete that was not available to anybody else."[4] Each side of the LP – the second volume of The Mole Trology – reflected the music of two different cultures. The Chub side features a delicious cover version of Stan Kenton's million selling "Eager Beaver" masquerading as "Mousetrap". Similarly "Happy Home" sounds remarkably like Kenton's "Machito".

The Residents soon realised that by judicious use of a couple of Emulators they could not only play live, but rather than produce a poor imitation of their recorded selves, they could take the authentic Residents' sound out on the road with them, stored on computer disc.

The next step was to set about planning what kind of show they were going to put on. They had no interest in presenting some kind of rock 'n' roll performance. They envisaged something operatic and spectacular. *The Mark of The Mole* material was ideal for a type of theatrical presentation. The LP, released in 1981 as the first part of a trilogy, had been an ambitious, serious-minded concept inspired by the Great Depression of the 1930s that dealt with the friction between two cultures after natural disaster had forced one – "the Moles" – to migrate to the land of another culture – "the Chubs". Dealing with the problems of assimilation, exploitation and inevitably conflict, all of this was ripe to be acted out on stage using a variety of props, backdrops and musical accompaniment. As Hardy Fox explained:

> "It's more of a theatrical presentation. A group of dancers will be acting out the story... and The Residents will be in a sort of booth at the back of the stage playing the music. Except for the Overture, the intermission music and the finale, which will be taped, all the music will be done live, and it will be overwhelmingly keyboards, although there will probably be a couple of guitars as well.."[5]

The Residents set to work planning and constructing a show. They set themselves no financial constraints; they didn't need to. Up to 30th September 1980, Ralph Records had raked in, before expenses, over $500,000. On the face of it this looks a lot but it should be borne in mind that this was based on sales alone and did not take into consideration any expenses, i.e. manufacturing cost of records, purchase of musical equipment, living expenses, salaries, servicing the Grove Street mortgage, taxes etc. It should also be noted that these figures covered all the sales from 1972. This was not simply one year's income. Still, it was a nice tidy sum.

The Residents thought more about what they were going to put into the show rather than what they were going to get out of it. The Cryptic Corporation went along with all this expecting that the show would comfortably pay for itself.

Grove Street became a workshop where 21 huge 18 foot backdrops were designed by Poreknowgraphics and painted by a legion of workers. Costumes were designed and props – full size Moles and Chubbs were crafted into shape. The Residents rehearsed for the concert with two Emulators and full technical backup from E-MU systems who were gratified to have their technology showcased. (Indeed, they even named their Research and Development room after The Residents.) Slowly the show came together.

They advertised for dancers at a local studio. Carol Lemaitre recalls; "The audition notice was pretty bizzare... Avant-garde band needs dancers. Possible European tour."[6]

Sarah McLennan, her dancing partner: "Dancers are notoriously unfamiliar with music, especially modern music, and I don't think any of them recognised who The Residents were apart from me and a couple of other people."[7]

They both went over to the studio. It was, "Obviously not a dance studio. These guys were standing around."[8]

The audition was run by Kathleen French who was choreographing the show on behalf of The Residents. It was a typical dance audition. She taught the movement and the several dancers who had bothered to show up followed it. At the end of the day four were hired to dance on the tour.

To make things clear for anybody attending the show who might have been unfamiliar with the obscure Mole concept, The Residents decided to use a narrator, who at suitable junctures in the performance would explain what was going on. Penn Jillete had come to their attention with his partner Teller during the long running madcap *Asparagus Valley* revue in San Francisco. Jillette's first task was to record the hilarious *Ralph Records 10th Anniversary Radio Special* where he was locked in a Motel room for six days and forced to endure all of the Resident/Ralph releases. As for his role in the Mole show:

"I was handed a script from a word processor that had all the lyrics to all the songs, what the songs were about, an absract description of the dances... and then the spaces for what I was supposed to do."[9]

His job...

"...just coming out and essentially talking in those sections – which had times on them incidently – a minute, two minutes. Do a minute and a half here, get irritated here, go crazy and so on and you'll be tied up here.."[10]

Jillette was basically a one man Greek chorus and as a comedian would inject some humour into what Homer Flynn promised to be a "reasonably intense" show. More importantly it also allowed the performance to project some personality. The Residents intended to remain behind a netted screen at the back of the stage in keeping with their reticent reputation.

Even the lighting was to be different from the norm. This was entrusted to Phil Perkins, a cinematographer who had helped light *Hello Skinny* and the *One Minute Movies*:

"I thought from the beginning that I did not want it to look like a current rock concert. At that time (1981), people lit rock concerts with hundreds of parcams and it just seemed to me like the shotgun approach. That's not lighting, that's illumination. Just turn the switches on and kaboom! You flash the blue ones, then you flash the red ones and turn on the smoke machine and that's considered lighting. Well, that's ridiculous."[11]

As "It was suppose to be a dark, powerful, operatic type of show," Perkins lit it accordingly. "Rock shows tend to be lit like old fashioned television, the lighting is frontal and high. We lit our show back and low."[12] There was one spotlight to illuminate Jillette for his walk-on parts.

The cost of the Mole Show was colossal. No expense was spared. Including The Residents there would be some thirteen people on stage – four dancers (slimmed to three in Europe), Jillette and four backdrop movers. There was also the lighting and sound people as well as the roadies. By the time it toured Europe it was around 20 people strong. The Residents did not care. To them, this was not merely a series of live performances but an artistic showcase of everything they stood for. Music, art and theatre rolled into one.

The first performance of the Mole Show was a low-key warm-up gig at The House in Santa Monica, southern California, on the 10th April, 1982. None of the dancers or props were involved, it was merely intended to run some of the music through its paces. The Residents played behind a transluscent white sheet in a totally darkened room to an audience of sixty or so people. The show went well with no real problems. Six months later – October 26th – the Mole Show officially opened with two sold-out shows in the Kabuki Theatre in San Francisco and then played four shows in Los Angeles and one in Pasadena.

The shows were well received by the audiences. Jillette's acid narration – "That was real flashy in a low tech sort of way" – perfectly diffused any thoughts of pretentiousness on the part of the performance. Some reviewers obviously had difficulty with the theatrical concept, but did not conceal their approval even if it was grudgingly given.

At the Pasadena show, The Residents had their first brush with rock 'n' roll petulance. They were on a double bill with Wall of

Voodoo who, at the time, were on the brink of MTV fuelled one-hit wonderdom. It had been agreed in advance that The Residents would "headline" the show and therefore perform last. (After all, it was Halloween). However, as show time approached, Wall of Voodoo decided that they didn't want to play second fiddle to a bunch of wackos droning on about a load of fucking Moles. Call that Rock 'n' Roll? They dug in their leather-booted heels and insisted on playing last. When approached with this "problem", The Residents were blasé. "This band with guitars and drums want to go on after the Mole Show?" said one Resident, "Sure, we'll go first." When this was related to Wall Of Voodoo, however, they changed their minds. Either they feared, in rock parlance, being "blown off the stage" or felt a sudden compassion for their loyal headbanging fans. The Residents closed the show.

With these first concerts negotiated without any major problems apart from a tendency for the Emulator disc drives to overheat – there were 85 disc changes throughout the show – the following May, The Residents took the Mole Show to Europe and into the teeth of a disaster.

The European tour was in many respects a double-sided coin. The performances went well and were enthusiastically received by sell-out audiences and reviews were more favourable from the open-minded critics. However, the tour lost a bundle of money.

There had been some financial worries from The Cryptic Corporation before the "troupe" flew to Europe. There was a staggering amount of props and backdrops to transport and the travel cases were so large that they could only fit in the hold of a 747. It cost a tremendous amount of money to fly them across. Then there was the number of people involved – two dancers were shed to cut costs – some 20 people had to be fed and watered and put up in hotels. However, they were told by their newly signed business manager Bill Gerber (who at the time managed the much touted Devo, The Cars and Tom Petty amongst others) not to worry. They would recoup all of their expenses and outlay when selling out in Europe. Of course, this was not the case. Even though the European tour was a sold-out success they still lost money at the end of the day. A lot of money. Why?

Firstly, there was no large record company behind the band to pick up the tab for staging such an extravagant show. The Cryptic Corporation, Ralph Records and ultimately The Residents themselves had to pick up the bills. In order to generate some much needed cashflow, before the tour got under way, the Cryptic Corporation sold the merchandising rights for the entire tour for some $10,000. This included Poreknowgraphics' original designs for T-shirts and other promotional material. At every concert this "official" Residents merchandise sold like hot cakes. The Residents did not see a cent over the agreed figure.

Although at this time, the sale of promotional items at concerts was not as big a business as it is today, it is ironic that the Cryptic Corporation sold the rights, considering that up until that point in their career they had maintained a very strong hands-on policy towards merchandising. Their own T-shirts and other promotional materials had sold strongly through their well established mail order operation. They even had their own full time "hawker" in Tom Timony on tour with them, and if they had manufactured and sold their own products, the tour would not have ended as a financial disaster. Of course, talking from hindsight is easier than dealing with the reality. At the time, the tour was underfunded and the $10,000 offer of cash in advance for the merchandising rights seemed too juicy a carrot to refuse. It was something they didn't have to worry about.

A major factor in the disaster could be attributable to the departure of Jay Clem and John Kennedy from The Cryptic Corportation. From the outset Clem had been the mouthpiece of the organisation and his departure in July 1982 was a big blow. The reason for his departure is, even now, rather unclear, although there were rumours of personality clashes and one source suggests that he "Got frustrated with the biz. I think he wanted to be a big businessman. A powerbroker."[13] Perhaps he was tired of petty hassles with distributors, having to continually chase them for monies owed and wanted a bigger stage for his talents than that offered by Ralph Records. He may have merely felt it was time to move on. Whatever, for him, it was a traumatic experience.

> "Things have been really insane for some time now. It's been really hard to function in the environment that developed around me... I'm leaving Ralph/Cryptic... It was very difficult and painful, and I think, the best for all concerned. I still love my partners and The Residents, et al."[14]

Clem was around long enough to help publicise the early dates of the Mole Tour and was speaking to journalists as late as October 1982. However, shortly after The Residents tenth Anniversary package was produced – custom made golf balls, pizza pan holders, Santa Dog sponge forehead thermometers and false locks of Residents' hair! – he bowed out to establish his own management company and, ironically, finally shattered the myth that he was a Resident once and for all.

His departure, however, left a hole. Of all of the Cryptic officials, Clem was the one most in touch with the music business. He was the one that had supervised the expansion of the label as well as negotiating most of the licencing agreements with European record labels. He had conducted most of the interviews with journalists.

Perhaps if he had remained with the Cryptics during the tour he could have used his obvious skill to try and minimise the financial problems. John Kennedy left shortly after the performances at the Kabuki Theatre in San Francisco, leaving Homer Flynn, the graphic designer, and Hardy Fox, sound technician to deal with the group's business affairs. Kennedy's timing could not have been worse. Over the years he had, "pumped a lot of money into the record company and the record company soaked up the money."[15]

However, with the discovery that the proposed Mole tour of Europe was underfunded and promising to consume even more money, he decided that enough was enough. In his eyes the project had run its course.

> "We were making some money. I would not say that we were profitable, certainly it was not paying back the purchase of the property... Once it (Ralph) had been set up it was managing to maintain a cashflow. It even required refinancing. We would borrow money to permit certain projects... We had done a decade of it and produced many recordings and a film had been attempted. That had been enough."[16]

Kennedy's departure was a body blow. Unlike Clem who in leaving took an agreed sum of money, the American rights to Yello and their first two LP's, after protracted negotiations with the remaining Cryptic officers, Kennedy acquired something much more valuable – 444 Grove Street:

> "I did not kick them out in any way but we had to establish a fair market value – rent agreement – which was above Ralph Records ability to pay."[17]

There was a reasonable notice period for Flynn and Fox, the remaining members of The Cryptic Corporation, to find a suitable alternative but it was traumatic for The Residents who believed that they would be in Grove Street "forever." They later moved into a building next to a freeway in Clementine Street, although due to restrictions on space, they had to jettison a huge amount of material including all of the costumes and sets from *Vileness Fats* as well as other beloved memorabilia in a huge "garage sale".

Once they got to Europe, as well as the financial problems, The Residents also had to deal with their notoriously hard-drinking English roadcrew. Used to handling rock bands with huge egos, groupies offering blow jobs and plenty of illegal substances, they found the low-key approach of The Residents tour party a real pain in the arse. They were none too pleased with having to wear grey boiler suits and fake Groucho Marx spectacle and moustache combinations like the rest of the touring party to protect the identities of The Residents. They also had a problem with Penn Jillette who was totally against smoking and drinking. Consequently the two European tour mini-buses became homes of rival factions, "The Party Bus" led by hard-drinking roadies "sweating gin" and "The Library Bus" led by Jillette. Those who did not belong to either faction floated amongst the two.

Resident/Roadie relations hit their nadir when the roadies pulled all the instrument patches at end of the prestigious Hammersmith Odeon concert in London, so that when The Residents attempted an encore there was no power and consequently no sound. It took over five minutes to prise the roadies away from their beer cans and grudgingly restore power so the band could play "Smack Your Lips". Of course, the tour was not all doom and gloom, even if there were road accidents, equipment thefts and Penn Jillette nearly dying in a Spanish hospital with a gastric complaint.

Nevertheless, for some of the people on the tour it was a great experience. It was a first look at Europe. As Carol Lemaitire states:

"We were not so much aware of the financial problems, so we were having a good time and the pressure was less on us as opposed to The Cryptic Corporation who were watching their childrens' life savings going down the drain. They weren't having so much fun."[18]

Looking back from the vantage point of 1993, Homer Flynn recalls:

"I think artistically it was very interesting, but financially it was totally disasterous and it took its emotional toll too. Really heavy... When you've never toured before and you go on the road with twenty people and lots of backdrops and stuff you find out why people take drugs in terrific loads!"[19]

After the last date at Leicester Polytechnic in England on July 1st, 1983, The Residents flew back to to America vowing never ever to tour again. They had been, "raped by promoters and killed on merchandise."[20] All they had to show from staging and presenting an ambitous piece of performance art were huge debts that were threatening to capsize their entire Ralph Records operation.

Ironically, succour from financial pressures came from an unexpected source – an offer to stage the Mole Show one last time at the opening night of the New Music America Festival in Washington DC. The Residents at first refused, but when the financial carrot got bigger they were not in a position to turn it down. It would clear some of their debts.

However, the consequences of the European tour haunted this show. All of their instruments had been confiscated by a shipping company in England for non-payment. Apparently, the tour manager had been supposed to pay the bill but never did – he, like the tour, had run out of cash. The dispute dragged on. The agent began escalating the asking price to send the equipment back until it reached $16,000. The Residents paid $10,000 and agreed to pay the balance after they played the Washington show. The agent accepted this first payment and then refused to send the instruments until he received the final $6,000. Meanwhile, showtime was slowly approaching.

To make matters worse, The Residents were supposed to be the curtain-raising act of the two-week festival that was staged in a different city each year. The Promoters had taken an "aesthetic gamble" by booking the band as their music was unlike anything else on the bill.

The Residents refused to tell the promoters, naively clinging to the belief that the shipping agent would eventually honour his word and everything would be alright. Phil Perkins recalls nearly pulling his hair out over this – "We arrived there with no instruments, no props, no sets and no costumes and had to break that to them"[21] – as far as he could see the show would have to be cancelled and he told The Residents this. He was told that, "We were going to do a show even if it meant standing out there in our underwear with a slide projector."[22]

Everything was built from scratch. Backdrops. Slides were made up to represent the backdrops that could not be made in time. Moles and Chubbs were constructed. A local ballet school was contacted to get young dancers to add colour. Attempts were made to get Penn Jillette to the show – airline schedules confounded him – in the end The Residents' manager played the protagonist. J.Raul Brody played Uncle Sam. Perkins recalls the mad rush to pull a show together:

> "...The band trying to rehearse the whole deal, rehearse the choreography in a couple of rooms in the local YMCA, and in the vacant lot next door there was this army of people from California

spray painting things and trying to build all the props on the street in time for the opening."[23]

There was also a problem of instrumentation. There was a "Statewide search for what, at the time, was very rare equipment; two emulators, programmable synths, standard stuff like basses, guitars.."[24] The Emulators were obtained only after The Cryptic Corporation rang EM-U Systems and got a local dealer to lend their demo model. Ironically, the equipment from England arrived hours before showtime. (Their manager, Bill Gerber, in England for a wedding, had gone and threatened the shipping agent). Two of The Residents went down to get their trademark eyeballs. The rest of the stuff was left there to be flown back to San Francisco. The show would go on. Phil Perkins:

"The dress rehearsal was just awful. Not only was it awful sounding, it broke down a couple of times. We couldn't even keep the show going. We had to stop."[25]

However on the night things were altogether different. Perkins again:

"The Residents came out and I think that they killed. Of all the Mole performances I was involved in, it was the most passionate, the most colourful, the most varied. Precise enough, but with something very dangerous and angry going on, which was what the Mole Show was all about."[26]

The show over, The Residents went back to California to lick their wounds. As for The Cryptic Corporation, it had the more pressing problem of keeping Ralph Records solvent.

Footnotes
1. Homer Flynn at The Museum of Modern Art. New York. 19th October 1992.
2. Phil Perkins. Interview with author. October 1992.
3. Brian Poole. Interview with Author.
4. J. Raul Brody. Interview with Author.
5. Hardy Fox to *Keyboard*, October 1982.
6. Carol Lemaitre. Interview with Author. October 1992.
7. Sarah MacLennen. Interview with Author. October 1992.
8. Carol Lemaitre. Interview with Author. October 1992.
9. Penn Jillette quotes from London Mole Show Press conference. June 1983.
10. Ibid.
11. Phil Perkins. Interview with Author. October 1992.
12. Ibid.
13. Tom Timony. Interview with Author. October 1992.
14. Jay Clem. Letter to Edwin Pouncey 17th July 1982.
15. Tom Timony. Interview with Author, October 1992.
16. John Kennedy. Interview with Author.
17. Ibid.
18. Carol Lemaitre. Interview with Author. October 1992.
19. Homer Flynn. October 19th, 1992.
20. Phil Perkins. Interview with Author. October 1992.
21. Ibid
22. Ibid.
23. Ibid.
24. Rich Shupe. Interview with Author. October 1992.
25. Phil Perkins. Interview with Author. October 1992.
26. Ibid.

POST MOLE RECOVERY

"Problems with the company after the Mole Show period – we really had to survive – we played to sold out audiences in Europe and came back broke."[1]

Tom Timony

In order to survive it was imperative to make money. The Uncle Sam Mole Show, for all of its tribulations, had at least brought in some much needed cash. More was raised by Tom Timony – now literally running Ralph Records with his wife Sheenah – selling a large amount of surplus stock to a cut price dealer. These records were sold for a fraction of their value but the money received helped with the cashflow at a critical time. It was not as if Ralph Records could sell these records to distributors or by direct mail order. By 1983 the bottom was fast falling out of the English and American independent scene. Ralph was struggling to survive.

Another source of revenue came through the sale of "rare" items. "New Ralph" was set up after Kennedy and Clem left the organisation. It was decided to make a clean start and rename Ralph Records; hence the New Ralph logo. No doubt there were also legal reasons. Anyway, the new mail order catalogue of April 1983 auctioned off items like one of the Asbestos suits used in early promo pictures (Minimum bid $150.00), a guitar "broken by a Resident on stage in Düsseldorf." (Minimum bid $300.00), "Resident signed" brown vinyl copies of *Mark of The Mole*, ($30.00 each), test pressings, old envelopes, posters, as well as a few "archive" copies of ultra rare Resident releases like "Santa Dog", "Babyfingers" and *Meet The Residents*. This policy of "auctioning off" limited amounts of the family silver to maintain cashflow would continue with subsequent mail order catalogues. Compilation albums also began to be released ranging from the excellent collection of unreleased material called *Residue* to the flaccid two volumes of *Ralph Before '84* which consisted of previously released material.

Fortunately, Ralph Records was able to rush-release another Residents LP. In fact this was a collaboration with fellow label mates Renaldo and The Loaf. The backing tracks had been laid down as early as March 1981 when Brian "Renaldo" Poole and Dave "Loaf" Janssen had visited Ralph Records shortly after being signed up. Brian recalls:

> "During our time there The Residents hinted that they thought it would be fun to see what happened if The Residents and Renaldo and the Loaf got into a studio space at the same time. We were excited about that, but because of the rehearsals going on at the time and other commitments, The Residents had left it to the last four days of our stay... It became very frantic. Everyone crammed into the studio space. Various jam sessions. Switching the tape on and seeing what would happen. The notion came about to see if a piece, or various pieces could be constructed in four days. It wasn't!"[2]

What they did end up with was a 45 minute master tape of various jam sessions upon which one of The Residents did a little post production work before putting it in the archive. However, after meeting Brian and Dave two years later backstage after the Mole Show at Hammersmith Odeon, London, talk fell to completing the tapes. Subsequently, Brian flew out to San Francisco in early September 1983 for three weeks to help complete the project. Dave Janssen could not get the time off work, so he sent some tape loops.

Upon arriving in San Francisco, Brian recalls being dissapointed that the instrumentation in the new studio at Clementine Street was pretty basic. He had hoped to get his hands on an Emulator, however, at this time all equipment used for the Mole tour was still in England. As for the recording session:

> "It was just a case of listening to (the original tapes) and using them as templates to build pieces on. In some instances the original stuff from the jam session comes through on the recordings, in some instances it has totally dissappeared and been replaced by something else."[3]

Like Chris Cutler before him, Brian recalls that The Residents stuck, "to a strict regime of working. Discipline. I just got weekends off."[4] For two weeks they came in at nine, broke for lunch at one and worked until six in the evening. Even an attack of influenza did not prevent the main vocalist from fulfilling his vocal chores. "I remember one Resident laying on the floor with the microphone next to him."[5] How sick this Resident was during this recording session can be heard on the track "Woman's Weapon". Poole recounts how the Resident performed when in rude health:

> "...the lyrics to the songs... were acted out at the same time... obviously not dancing around the studio but in front of the mike a definite emotion and gestures of emotion... over and above what a

singer would do to pump themselves up. Crouching down around the microphone and acting it out as if on stage."[6]

As to how they worked in their studio environment:

"Things were built up slowly. Ideas were pretty spontaneous. When they decided that a bit of Snakefinger would sound good here, they simply rang him up and he came down to the studio."[7]

The way Snakefinger approached recording was that, "He just came in and did them (his overdubs) all in one go. Just sat there and did it. First take. No messing."[8]

The finished LP – *Title in Limbo* – was released in November 1983 and was an interesting addition to The Residents canon. One review states that it did not sound like either of its parents and this is true. What is interesting about the collaboration is the accessibility of the music. It is very relaxed and pleasant to listen to. Acoustic hummable tunes. The Residents were obviously pleased with it. They even performed one of the outstanding tracks – "Monkey and Bunny" – on their 13th Anniversary tour. More importantly, the record sold well, helping to replenish the Ralph/Cryptic/Residential coffers. Renaldo and the Loaf bought an 8 track studio with their cut of the royalties.

As for the next Residents project, after the financial disaster of the Mole Tour they felt little desire to complete part three of the Mole Trilogy. They wanted to put that behind them and move onto something else. Therefore work commenced on an ambitious project that had been on the back boiler of their collective imagination for some time. This was to be their *American Composers Series*. The idea behind this was simple. The Residents would offer their own "phonetic" interpretations of the seminal music of various American composers. This would not simply be confined to "classical" music. In their eyes Captain Beefheart, Sun

Ra, Smokey Robinson, Harry Nillson and Bob Dylan were just as important as Charles Ives and Harry Partch.

In total The Residents intended to "cover" the works of no less than twenty composers over the next 16 years completing the entire project by 2001. Each LP release would feature the "music" of two composers; one on each side. A list was drawn up and work commenced.

The first fruit, released in March 1984, was *George and James*, where various keynote compositions of George Gershwin and James Brown were "interpreted". However, despite the interesting concept, the music was dissapointing. Gershwin classics like "Rhapsody in Blue", "I Got Rhythm" and "Summertime" were over-synthetic and flaccid in the extreme. There is none of the Residential chemistry at work that made their previous cover versions so individually strong and iconoclastic. As for the "James" side it was better – but not by much. Rather than play it safe and spotlight individual tracks from James Brown's long and varied career, The Residents boldly chose to cover the seminal *Live at the Apollo* album. Their re-working was abysmal. The music is sloppy, the vocals sounding as if they had been sung by someone in their sleep. There is no hint of the spark and vitality that made James Brown's music so successful. There is no energy, no funk, no show. The sound of a "live" audience – taken from the Mole Show in Holland – was as poor as the obviously "studio" constructed music. The cover art was more interesting than the music. Porknowgraphics' portraits of the two composers was his first dabbling with computer generated images.

The subsequent single – thankfully not taken from the LP – was much better. "It's A Man's World" is much more of a successful meeting between the Godfather of Soul and the Masters of the Underground. The ridiculously slowed, slurred vocals of the LP are abandoned in favour of a more typically Residential delivery. The stripped down synthesised music is more imaginatively realised. The packaging was excellent – the first 4,000 were released on white vinyl and featured a large iris in the centre, so the single resembled the trademark eyeball icon.

The most interesting product of the *George and James* material was the video. This was financed by Warner Brothers to promote the LP and single in Western Europe. The generous budget allowed The Residents to rent a studio for a day and shoot some live action footage with Phil Perkins. (Their new premises were much too small to use as a film set). They also acquired a video computer upon which they constructed animated segments.

The completed video was fantastic, eyeballed Residents in white tuxedos walk nervously backwards through what looks like a forest of smoking stove-like ovens. For the filming of the live action segment, The Residents wore the trademark tuxedo and eyeball combination. It was so hot under the studio lights and inside the plastic eyeball that one of them fainted. As for the animated footage, a grey-faced Resident with flashing Medusa-like orange hair sings out of synch. Absolutely fantastic computer images perfectly shadow the lyrics of the song; cars dissolving into ships into money etc. As well as being shown in Europe, the video received limited exposure on MTV.

This was a shame as the video showcased The Residents tremendous visual flair at a time when there was a boom in the use of video to promote music. By 1984, music video had taken off to the extent that it was becoming de rigueur for singles to be accompanied by a promotional video. Like Devo, The Residents had somewhat anticipated this trend – *Vileness Fats*, *Land of 1,000 Dances*, *Hello Skinny* and the *One Minute Movies* – but were no longer in a position to exploit the medium. The main outlet (in

America) was the now hugely successful MTV which was only interested in showing hit videos, hit songs and established artists. There was very little scope for the promotion of videos from outside the mainstream. True, innovative video imagery could and did break hit singles and new acts, but they usually reflected a certain type of music and visual style. Experimental video by cult artists still got about as much public exposure as a monk's genitals.

The fact that they were on the outside looking in had never bothered The Residents, but there was no escaping the fact that they were no longer in a strong enough financial position to finance their own promotional videos for themselves and other Ralph acts. The Mole Show disaster and decline of the independent music scene in England and America effectively scuppered the idea of attempting to build Ralph into a large, flourishing independent record company with a wide range of acts. Additional staff who had been taken on during Ralph's expansion to deal with areas like art direction and promotion, had to leave the company. There simply wasn't the money to pay them. True, "New Ralph" did retain a small roster of other acts and experimented with new releases by Rhythm and Noise, Nash the Slash, Hajime Tachibana and others. However, these were conspicuously one-off affairs and henceforth Ralph concentrated mainly upon the act that had contributed to their success –The Residents.

The Residents themselves were still brimming with ideas, but hampered by limited resources. If they were going to continue to express visual ideas on film/video then they would have to find "sponsorship" from other sources. Try to sell art to business.

With this in mind, The Residents floated a proposal to produce a series of "Science Fiction's Greatest Hits" where original footage from 1950's science fiction movies would be coloured, edited and enhanced with computer graphics. The end product would be a series of short two to four minute long featurettes which could be shown on TV, MTV or released on video cassette. All the accompanying music would be provided by The Residents.

With a view to soliciting funding for this project, The Residents produced a demonstration tape. The 1956 film *Earth Vs. The Flying Saucers* was treated accordingly. The results were visually stunning and created something totally original. Negotiations took place with interested parties in the film industry but a deal could not be struck. There was a problem with copyright as most of the films were owned by different studios and it would be too expensive to buy the rights to them all. The original music for *Earth Vs. The Flying Saucers* was given away as a free one-sided single with the first edition of the 1986 *Cryptic Guide to The Residents* – an updated version of the 1981 fan club book.

The Residents had always been keen to work on film soundtracks, however most producers found their music "too weird" and therefore avoided using them. Eventually, in 1985 they were finally commissioned to score a feature film, a low budget horror flick called *The Census Taker*. The Residents were not the first choice for the project. Indeed, by the time they got involved, two soundtracks had already been commissioned and rejected. At the eleventh hour they were recommended to the producers of the film by their friend, the comedian Penn Jillette.

The commission was hardly ideal. Time restraints allowed very little original material to be recorded and the bulk of the soundtrack came from selective editing of existing recordings like the *Commercial Album*. Ironically, when completed the film never received a general release. It finally came out on video. The Residents liked the soundtrack but did not think much of the film. There have been, as yet, no subsequent commissions.

In the three years since the release of the *Tunes Of Two Cities* in 1982 there had been a rash of supplementary releases associated with the Mole series, all proclaiming that they were not the third and final instalment of the Trilogy. There had been the Intermission music played during the tour, a live LP, a low quality video recording as well as official and unofficial bootlegs of Mole Show concerts.

There had even been a series of comic books produced independently by the illustrator and fan, Matt Howarth. These *Comix of Two Cities* were based around the fictional Mole characters. Matt Howarth:

> "I originally did the first issue of *The Comix Of Two Cities* as a tangent of silliness which I felt compelled to pursue upon hearing The Residents *The Tunes Of Two Cities*. That first issue made its debut at The Residents San Francisco concert in the early '80s, and was swiftly followed by five more issues of the comic, co-published Howski Studios and Ralph Records."[9]

A limited edition was even produced in German! The complete story ran to 12 issues and although issues 7-12 were completed they were never published. Howarth is a comic book artist with a unique and individual graphic style and fertile imagination. In order to "bridge the comic book field with the field of alternative music"[10], he also featured The Residents as well as other favourite musicians in a large number of his excellent, amusing and continuing *Savage Henry* series.

In October 1985, The Residents finally released the next instalment in the Mole Trilogy. This was not, as expected, part three but part four! The Residents had perversely decided rather than finishing the project in three parts to extend it to six – parts one, three and five being political, parts two, four and six were social. This fourth part was entitled *The Big Bubble* and at the time of its release, the cover artwork caused a great stir because it featured four men in white tuxedos with their faces exposed, leading many to think that The Residents had finally got sick of their anonymity and revealed themselves. This was another Residential hoax. The four people on the front cover were not The Residents but actors who had been hired to portray a mythical "band" called The Big Bubble that had grown out of the union between the Moles and the Chubs. As for the music it was intended to be a series of short Mole/Chub-like garage songs. In fact, it sounded as if The Residents were painfully exorcising the demons of the entire Mole Show debacle. Songs like "Gotta Gotta Get" and "Go Where Ya Wanna Go" are disturbing cries of naked emotional pain.

This was enhanced by the way the album was recorded:

> "The vocalist would sing the song first without instruments or rhythm and the arrangements would be worked out on that improvised structure. The timing of the singing is very erratic, so it required laying like a grid behind the vocal to find the points where things would fall."[11]

The entire LP is dominated by cries, shrieks, groans and a whole host of other vocal effects. Some of it works, whilst a large part borders on the self-indulgent with its repetition of nonsensical babbling and vocal histrionics. Some fans loved it but many remained less than keen.

For the first time in their career The Residents sounded as if they were treading water. Perhaps it was their increasing dependence upon the Emulator, sampling and synthesiser technology that seemed to bland out the rough edges that had always personalised their music. Perhaps they were simply getting tired of continually working in the studio producing music. Perhaps it was having to deal with the real world and the financial pressures brought on by the problematic Mole tour. Perhaps they simply needed a new challenge.

Footnotes
1. Tom Timony. Interview with Author. October 1992.
2   Brian Poole. Interview with Author. August 1992.
3   Ibid.
4   Ibid.
5   Ibid.
6   Ibid.
7   Ibid.
8   Ibid.
9. Matt Howarth. Letter to the Author.
10. Ibid.
11. Hardy Fox to *Sonics*, November 1986.

© MATT HOWARTH

13th ANNIVERSARY

"It's hot. It's terribly hot. You can see. There's a scrim, a little black scrim on the pupil that allows you to see out, but it's really hot, but they also have this strange acoustic thing happening inside because you're in this goldfish bowl so there's this reverberation when people are speaking to you..."[1]

Rex Ray

After the Mole Show debacle, The Residents had decided never to tour again. However, early in 1985 they were approached by Wave records, their Japanese label, with an offer to tour Japan. At first, The Residents were not interested and cited the financial and emotional cost of the *Mole* tour as the principal reasons. Wave, however remained persistent, and more importantly offered to bear all financial responsibilities; airfare, hotel accommodation, performance payments and shipment of all instruments and props. It was a juicy carrot and slowly The Residents began to sniff at it:

"...there was some contemplation, itching about doing it, because it was the one thing that The Residents had never really mastered. They had this whole studio thing down, they had all the visuals down, they had conquered all their anonymity problems and so on, but touring was one thing they were not completely certain about."[2]

Finally, they took the carrot. With everything paid for they could hardly refuse. They set about creating an economical performance they would be comfortable with. There was no talk of backdrops, narrators, props and playing some heavy conceptual music. Rather, they decided to make this short Japanese tour a musical celebration of 13 years of activity featuring material from their vast back catalogue. Music recorded in the studio but never played live. They also decided to take Snakefinger with them.

Of course, with The Residents there had to be some kind of floorshow. As well as having the traditional focal point of a Lead Singer who would go through a variety of costume changes, there were the two Resident dancers. They too would go through a variety of costume changes, as well as using lightweight hand-held props and inflatable giraffes. As for the lighting this would be minimal and revolved around the creative use of car/loft inspection lamps. The Residents set about programming their synths, rehearsing and getting ready to fly out and put on a show.

It was at this time that Rich Shupe appeared on the scene. Shupe had been a long time fan from the age of thirteen and had heavily featured the music of his heroes on his weekly college radio programme. Like many hardcore fans he began to persistently pester Ralph Records for information on The Residents and forthcoming releases. Over time he built up an ongoing mail and telephone relationship with John Kennedy who fielded most of his calls.

In April 1982, when Snakefinger's third LP *Manual of Errors* came out, Shupe rang Ralph with a view to doing a radio special on the guitarist and other new releases. He was informed that Snakefinger was going to tour to promote the record and in his enthusiasm Shupe found himself offering to promote Snakefinger's concert in Baltimore. He even went as far as to put the band up at his parents' house:

> "The whole band came to my house and we had like a barbeque and everything. Snakefinger did some laundry... and lost one of his socks in the dryer. He's at the gig getting ready and he says, 'I seem to have lost one of my favourite socks, can you check and see if it is at home?' So, I mailed it back to Ralph and they thought that was the funniest thing in the world, that Snakefinger's sock arrives in the mail from this fan. So I called the next week or something and said, 'Is John Kennedy there – talking to him in my monthly report – and Hardy (Fox) answered, who rarely answered the 'phone and said, "I know you, you're the one that mailed Snakefinger's sock!"[3]

That was the friendly nudge that got Shupe accepted by the Cryptic Corporation and the relationship was cemented when he helped paint backdrops and assisted with security for the Uncle Sam Mole Show in Washington.

When he rang up and was told about the dates in Japan, an obvious thought struck him; "If you've got something you can put on an airplane and take to Japan why can't you put it on a bus and take it to America?"

He then boldly offered to attempt to try and put "something" together in the two and a half weeks that The Residents were away in Japan. The Residents agreed to review the situation when they returned.

The short Japanese tour was hugely successful. The Residents were well treated by Wave who spared no expense and even constructed a huge sculpture in their record store in honour of The Residents' visit. They even arranged a few live TV appearances and on one of these The Residents performed their interpretation of "Jailhouse Rock". The four live performances in Kyoto and Tokyo were exceptionally well received and, more importantly, The Residents enjoyed performing them.

As for Shupe's activities when they returned, "there were far more shows than they ever wanted to do available to them."[4] After making the decision to tour America, The Residents set about pruning down the list and establishing an itinerary. They also wanted Shupe to manage the tour. This presented Shupe with a dilemma. Not only had he never managed a tour before but was also an undergraduate at college. Managing the three month tour would mean missing two college terms. It was a hard choice but with only one possible outcome. The Residents were his favourite band. At 19 he became their tour manager and the next three months were to be, for him, a "non stop thrill".

Unlike the Mole Show, everything about this tour was based upon strict economics. Everything – musicians, dancers, tour manager, equipment and props were all crammed into one large touring recreational vehicle. Again, unlike the Mole experience there were no factions and no English roadies!, "It was not luxurious by any means. It was more like a big family thing... The bathroom was full of equipment!"[5] The only problem with the travelling arrangements was Snakefinger's addiction to nicotine and other smouldering substances which saw him frequently disappear to the back of the bus so as not to annoy the majority who were non-smokers. For him, this was an enjoyable time and he was much loved by the other performers. He was, "just a really fabulous person... just his dignity on the road. That was his life and that was his home; travelling."[6]

Unlike the Mole performances, the 13th Anniversary tour was much looser. The emphasis was upon playing music and having fun rather than trying to project some huge musical concept piece. Hardy Fox:

"They started with the Mole Show because they started feeling like they were falling into a routine. The studio that had been their freedom had become their jail... All the freedom and ease of work, with time to try this and that and experiment, got so it wasn't satisfying because it wasn't scary enough. They felt they should be on stage in a situation where there was real time and to see what they could do and what would come out of it. Even after the Mole Show, they felt they were still too removed because that show was a theatrical piece. They thought they would try the club scene to see what that would be like and they're not trying to make any statements of any type."[7]

The "singing" Resident, stifled somewhat performing behind a scrim on the Mole tour, revelled in being the focal point of the show and made great play of wearing a wide range of teasing disguises that almost revealed his identity to the audience; wigs, false ears and a variety of tantalising masks.

The two Resident dancers also wore a variety of costumes including the full white tuxedos and eyeball regalia. Dancing in the eyeballs was problematic as there was a, "very small line of vision, no vision down, you can't see your feet or four foot in front of your feet." There was also, "no oxygen in these eyeballs... very heavy and no way to breathe."[8] When on stage they found that they could perform inside them for a maximum of twenty minutes. Unlike the Mole show, the two dancers had much more input into the choreography. The Residents gave them vague dynamic direction rather than specifics and let them work things out for themselves. There was, "a trust in the performers and also an interest in what chance will give you... Let's take these people, put them together, give this limited direction and see what we come up with and call it a piece."[9]

The tour was a great success. The Residents played in New York for the first time and their two shows at The Ritz were huge sell-outs. Indeed, at the time (1985), The Residents were the third biggest grossing show after Jerry Garcia and Eric Clapton. This time, there was also a firm hand on promotional merchandising. At the three sold-out San Francisco shows, Tom Timony hawked a stock of 106 different Residents items and nearly sold out of everything, much to the surprise of the concert promoters. As the tour progressed there were one or two venues The Residents should not have played; for instance a pool hall in Lawrence, Kansas near the local University. "You got twelve people clustered at the front while people were playing pool and ordering drinks at the back."[10] At another venue in the Midwest, The Residents played what was to be the venue's last concert. The next night the promoter was going to tranform it into a "Gentleman's Sports Bar" with female topless basketball.

Once the American tour was completed there was a six month break and then the show moved onto Australia, New Zealand and then into Europe. Again learning from past mistakes, it was done in the most economical way possible. Each performer having to carry one suitcase of props with their own luggage. Strict budgetary restrictions. At the end of the tour "The whole thing made a pretty good sum of profit... it was a financial success, the exact opposite experience of the Mole Show."[11]

As for the music on the show it was a collection of "classic" Residents' songs. "Lizard Lady", "Semolina", "Hello Skinny" and "Constantinople" from *Duck Stab/Buster and Glen*, were all radically restructured for performance and played mainly by one Resident resplendent in a skull mask. (His eyeball was stolen after the Los Angeles show on December 26th, 1985). He played behind a bank of Emulator sampling technology. Even "Smelly Tongues" from *Meet The Residents* and "Ship's A 'Going Down" from *Not Availiable* and "Walter Westinghouse" from the *Babyfingers* EP got a live airing. There was also some material from the recently released *The Big Bubble*.

Most important was the musical contribution of Snakefinger to the proceedings. As most of the music was synthesised, sampled and rigourously structured, his uniquely individual searing guitar parts and subtle accompaniment gave the show tremendous excitement and strength. The Residents obviously enjoyed playing with him live on a protracted basis and the feeling was warmly reciprocated. Although he always had to be on his toes. Snakefinger:

> "The Residents... don't believe in timing. I'm a career musician basically, everything I play in any band has very obvious timing and you know where you are. So, it's a little tricky with The Residents at first... you have to have a certain amount of telepathy going on. There is no logical timing. No four counts."[12]

As for the audiences, their response, especially in San Francisco, New York and Europe, was hugely enthusiastic. In many respects, this was the show they had wanted to see all along. The Residents playing live some of their favourite recordings.

As with The Mole Show, a live LP (recorded at one of the Japanese dates) was released with a fantastic cover by Japanese artist Tiger Tateishi. However, this did not feature all of the songs played on the tour and Ralph later released a limited edition double cassette and CD of the entire Minneapolis show. There was also a CD featuring music from the show in Amsterdam.

Footnotes
1. Interview with Author. October 1992.
2. Rich Shupe. Interview with Author. October 1992.
3. Ibid.
4. Ibid.
5. Ibid.
6. Carol LeMaitre. Interview with Author. October 1992.
7. Hardy Fox to *Now* Vol 5, No 20, Jan 23rd, 1986.
8. Sarah Mclennen. Interview with Author. October 1992.
9. Ibid.
10. Sarah Mclennen. Interview with Author. October 1992.
11. Rich Shupe. Interview with Author. October 1992.
12. Snakefinger to *Sonics*, November 1986.

STARS AND HANK

"I have one approach to playing the guitar... and that's to be that familiar with it and that good that I can play anything and not be bound within any tight time structure. I'm working towards that. And... trying to keep the random thing happening so I'm not so familiar that I know what I'm going to do all the time."[1]

Snakefinger

"Knowing Snakefinger and his sense of humour as we did, it is a fitting piece of irony that the very day of his death was also the day of the release of his new single, aptly entitled, "There's No Justice In Life."[2]

Ralph Record press release

We miss him, but know he continues to live in his music and our minds."[3]

Ralph Records, The Cryptic Corporation, & The Residents.

With their second tour completed The Residents went back into the studio to work upon the second part of their *Great American Composers Series* based around the music of the Country musician Hank Williams and the composer John Philip Sousa.

Entitled *Stars and Hank Forever*, the LP was a schizophrenic affair. The Hank side was an absolutely fantastic realisation of some of Williams' classic songs. Each "cover" is an absolute gem. "Hey Good Lookin", "Six More Miles to the Graveyard", "Ramblin' Man" and "Jambalaya" are excellent. The strength of the Hank Williams project was demonstrated by the fact that there were no less than three songs recorded but not used from the sessions; "Dear Brother", "Pictures of Life's Other Side" and "I'm So Lonesome I could Cry". All are to be found on the fan club CD *Daydream B-Liver* (UWEB 005). However, the outstanding track of those that did make it onto the LP was undoubtedly the discofied "Kaw Liga" which was justifiably released as a single.

It starts with a typical touch of Residential humour, a plundered sample of the opening bars of Michael Jackson's "Billie Jean" – a sly reference to the fact that Williams' wife shared the same name – then a drum machine takes over the beat and a powerful electric guitar comes in. The vocals are rich and straight from the swamps of Shreveport. The single went down so well in European nightclubs that a 12" four track "house mix" was released.

The entire Hank side is tremendously mainstream and the most instantly accessible and commercial music The Residents had ever released. It also marked a move towards using more traditionally sampled instruments rather than self-created sounds. They had tired of incorporating exotic and unusual sounds just for the sake of it. As Hardy Fox explained:

> "They sampled everything when they first got it (the Emulator). But once samplers became common and the exotic charm of having one was gone, they moved away from it. They've started going for traditional instrument sounds, very high quality digital sounds. They get professionals to record the sounds they want."[4]

The only problem was the other side of the LP. It was quite a jolt to flip the disc over and have to sit through twenty three minutes of classic American marching music. It was not as if the Sousa side was poorly realised – it was extremely well done – just that it presented such a stark contrast. Of course, this could have been The Residents intention. To offer two extremes of music to the listener and challenge his or her preconceptions. They certainly believed Sousa justified being covered. Hardy Fox:

> "He's one of the most solid, totally American composers there is. He was a true original. He virtually invented American patriotic music, and during his lifetime he was The Beatles; he was the most popular musician of his time. He's like the counterpart to Stravinsky."[5]

However, most reviews were in the rock press, who had no time for classical music and treated the LP as if it were two separate releases, strongly responding to Williams but lukewarm towards Sousa; "Get it for this side of Hank..."[6] "Just for God's sake don't turn it over."[7]

Stars and Hank sold strongly on the strength of the Hank side. The single sold well, although there was no money for a promotional video to try and push it into the heartland of the mainstream. Which was a shame. If anything was going to ferry The Residents across the waters into uncharted territory, it would have been "Kaw-Liga". Then again, as always, they had no interest in being anything but themselves.

Sadly, *Stars and Hank* was to be the last release in the *American Composers* series. The Residents did not lose interest in it, as they did the projected six volume Mole "cycle", but were overtaken by technology. By 1987 the CD revolution had literally wiped out vinyl as the main format upon which music was released in America. This meant that the idea of putting two performers, one on each side of an LP was negated. It simply could not be done on CD.

One composer would have to follow another. It would not work. Secondly, and more significantly, the advent of the CD had led to a rush of reissues and therefore revised royalty agreements for previously released material. If The Residents were to continue with this project they would have to pay quite high royalties to the composers of the original songs. As sales of their releases were relatively low (from *George and James* onwards in the region of 20,000 - 50,000) it would be financially unfeasible.

The next scheduled *American Composers Series* release - *The Trouble With Harry's* – reinterpreting the music of Harry Partch and Harry Nillson was abandoned. Tapes of early work upon some Sun Ra covers – notably "Space is the Place" – were also regretfully shelved.

In general, however, the abandonment of the *American Composers Series* was no great loss. True, it would have been interesting to see what The Residents would have done to the music of people like Stevie Wonder, Barry White, Scott Joplin or Captain Beefheart – they certainly had the vocalist for the latter – but it would have been time consuming and probably would have prevented them from composing and recording original material. In any event, they continued recording selected cover versions in the future.

Stars and Hank not only marked the end of the *American Composers Series* it also marked (with the 13th Anniversary show LP release) the end of the Cryptic Corporation's control of Ralph Records. The Cryptics no longer wanted to run a record company and mail order business and so handed Ralph Records lock stock and barrel over to Tom Timony and his wife Sheenah (who were running it anyway) for nothing. As well as receiving all the liabilities Timony's newly formed "T.E.C Tones" was also allowed to use the name Ralph Records for five years.

Snakefinger's contribution to the Hank Williams project had been some typically searing guitar licks on "Hey, Good Lookin'". Regretfully, this was to be the last time he worked with The Residents. Whilst touring Europe to promote his fifth solo LP *Night Of Desirable Objects* he had a fatal heart attack and passed away in his sleep on the night of 1st July, 1987. He was 38 years old.

Snakefinger had always had a heart problem. A heart attack in Australia in 1980 had put him in hospital for six months. However, his condition did not prevent him from pursuing the life he wished to lead. In some respects, he did not look after himself. He was continually smoking and never followed special dietary instructions.

By all accounts he was a very easy going friendly person. Quiet spoken. Courteous. "A true guy. Really sincere."[8] A musician to his fingertips. He could not imagine any other life than the one he led and his condition made him pursue it with even more gusto. He had taken up residence in San Francisco and loved the city. Whenever he came over to England he would meet up with Edwin Pouncey and tell him, "how great it was to live in San Francisco as he would never have to suffer another bloody London winter." Ironically his home in San Francisco was The Residents old Sycamore Street address.

Of course, despite his solo career he always existed in The Residents' shadow. This was no fault of theirs. It was just that his unique guitar sound was so much associated with some of their most seminal recordings. Snakefinger recorded his first two LPs in conjunction with The Residents who played, produced and assisted in composition. The resulting *Chewing Hides The Sound* (1979) and *Greener Postures* (1980) are both excellent. He then went on to record with his own band and subsequent tours and releases established his own musical personality. He indulged the more

Jazzy sounding side of his guitar playing on two releases with the Clubfoot Orchestra. His most ambitious project was his *History of the Blues*. As J.Raul Brody, who played piano on the tour and the LP release explained:

> "He was going through a phase where he was tired being pigeon-holed as an avant-garde musician and really wanted to do something a lot more earthy and emotional than the music he was notorious for. So he put together this ten piece blues band – no synthesisers, no electronics, no fancy stuff – all traditional blues... and demonstrated what a fantastic guitarist he was. He really copped the style of each of the blues artists he was covering."[9]

Phillip "Snakefinger" Lithman was buried in London. Edwin Pouncey attended the funeral and recalls it being a "Foul, horrible, shitty day" and had the strong feeling that "...he wasn't glad to be back really". Due to the distance involved The Residents did not attend the funeral but paid their own tribute by holding a musical wake to their lost friend. In black they played a heartfelt rendition of Williams' "Six More Miles To The Graveyard" and a series of renditions of old English laments. Several large black balloons were filled with helium, wrapped in black netting and attached to a number of tiny momentos brought forward by Snakefinger's friends. It was then symbolically released into the Heavens. Hardy Fox:

> "It was necessary to put an ending to a friend who died. When the balloons were released and disappeared it was like letting go of the period of grieving. It was time to go on with life and prepare to meet your own death at some point."[10]

Snakefinger was dearly missed by The Residents. He was a close personal friend first and a collaborator second. He left a hole that could simply not be filled. Edwin Pouncey:

> "When Snakefinger went, it was sort of like a real kind of blow to The Residents because they had lost one of the star attractions of the show... he just let rip with that guitar. It was extraordinary. He was not playing like, normal boring rock guitar he was playing something else. Very, very experimental."[11]

In his music, however, Snakefinger lives on.

Snakefinger had been pencilled in to contribute some guitar parts to The Residents next project, which was being finished at the time of his death, this was the ambitious spoken Opera, *God In Three Persons*. It was finally released in 1988 with guitar parts played by The Residents themselves. *God In Three Persons* saw The Residents returning to the conceptual arena and like *Hank* was a return to musical form. It is a spoken word opera or an "audio movie" with the musical accompaniment very much subservient to the strong, compelling visual narration. The "story" concerns Mr X Indeed, a Colonel Parker faith healing hustler, and his relationship with the young he/she freak he exploits/serves. It is a story of exploitation, lust, devotion and a whole heap more. More significantly it is also the first time that the poetic lyricism of The Residents had been properly presented. The spoken words are clear, rhythmic and easily understood. There is even an accompanying booklet of the lyrics for the listener to read as they listen.

Parts are extremely disturbing to listen to. Others are sensual. Laurie Amat, a woman gifted with extreme vocal qualities, collaborated with The Residents on parts of the recording and described listening to the master tapes as "...like watching an erotic movie... it made me cry. It was so sad". Her role in the story is to act as a "Greek Chorus" and also sing the opening credits at the beginning.

God In Three Persons split hardcore Residents' fans down the middle. Some loved it whilst others were annoyed that the constant voiceover detracted from the beautiful – just listen to those trombones! – music beneath. And it is true, the supporting music is exceptionally strong, all the old analogue synthesisers having been dragged out and dusted off. They made cunning use of the Swinging Medallions '60s hit "Doubleshot" – first covered on *Third Reich and Roll* – and the old hymn "Holy, Holy, Holy" ("God in three persons, beloved trinity") as recurring thematic motifs. Detractors were missing the point as the music was intended to compliment the narrative like a movie soundtrack. Of course, The Residents also released an LP of the soundtrack so everyone was satisfied.

Reviews were mixed although *Rolling Stone* described it as "no less than a Residential Tommy." In fact, *God In Three Persons* was the best original music that The Residents had produced for some time. As Cryptic spokesman Homer Flynn put it:

> "It's probably the most sophisticated thing they've done. In terms of impact, this is easily the strongest thing since *Eskimo* and *The Commercial Album* and maybe The Residents most powerful work of all."[12]

Interestingly enough, despite their love of technology, The Residents had been reticent to get involved with the advances offered by digital recording and computer generated music. One reason was expense, another was the fact that they were comfortable with their existing analogue 16 track Tascam machine. Laborious multi-tracking and tape splicing was an essential part of their sound – "There's virtually no tape that goes through the studio that doesn't get razor-bladed at some point", Hardy Fox explained. They were worried that by embracing direct digital recording, they would loose that hands-on ingredient that made their music so unique.

Circumstance however, had forced them to update their facilities in 1987, when they were commisssioned to score some episodes of Pee Wee Herman's Playhouse. Hardy Fox: "The first show had 81 cues and there was only a week to do them! You can't do that amount of work and expect to synch to video without a computer..."

Of course, once they dipped their toes in the water and found them warm they immersed themselves in this new recording technology and soon went totally MIDI. They also found writing music for TV was a whole new experience. Hardy Fox:

> "The Residents had to doctor things that had been written for a given episode to create music for other episodes. You can write one thing, then flop it around, change instruments, slow it down, and it becomes another cue. By the time they finished their third show – pulling their hair out because it really is work – they were developing pieces that became themes, little jingles, for things in the show. They were developing a language for visual expression. It was fascinating."[13]

God In Three Persons was envisioned as a CD only release (although it was eventually also released as a double LP). Despite the fact that the emergence of CD had helped to kill off the *Great American Composers* series, it was a medium they were eager to embrace due to its longer playing time and possibilities for thematic development. Hardy Fox:

> "With vinyl you think in terms of a strong start and a strong ending for each side. The CD presents an entirely different structure. You don't have to worry about whether you have too many long songs

on one side, or too many short ones on the other – especially since The Residents songs vary between a few seconds and several minutes long."[14]

The digital sound of the CD gave a greater clarity and brought out certain harmonics, especially in the remastering of their back catalogue that had not been evident on their initial vinyl release. Hardy Fox was delighted with the results; "It's great to hear the CDs sound so much like the master tapes. It's a real pleasure." Of course, this abandonment of vinyl had its downside. Hardy Fox:

"When we cut the records the engineer would photograph the grooves because he'd never seen anything like them before. He taught classes, and he'd use The Residents' work as classic examples of what you don't do."[15]

The entire Residents back catalogue was re-issued on CD with the addition of many rare and obscure tracks. East Side Digital handled the re-issues in America, whilst Torso did likewise in Europe.

God In Three Persons was an excellent and challenging concept piece. However, at this time The Residents' image was doing them no favours. Not only had the eyeball icon of the *Eskimo* period grown the wings of an albatross, but the entire self-generated Residents mythology had backfired in the sense that it had marginalised the music. The worst example of this occurred in *Reflex* Magazine which ran a huge feature on the *God In Three Persons* release. The journalist concerned simply blustered in a manner that must have had his obvious mentor, Lester Bangs, turning in his grave.

This was, however an extreme version of what had become a typical approach to The Residents' phenomenon. Features or reviews concentrating upon the theme of obscurists in tuxedos and plastic eyeballs on their heads. The music hardly got a crack and when it did it was always "weird" and "wacky." The Residents were becoming increasingly marginalised. Indeed, only the fact that they had commenced touring kept them in the public eye and won new converts outside of their devoted hardcore following for whom, in 1988, a new fan club – UWEB – was established. Uncle Willie's Eyeball Buddies was the second "official" Residents' fan club. Unlike the short lived W.E.I.R.D. (1978-81) it was established and run with The Residents' approval. Due to this there has been a regular flow of "members only" CD releases that range from rare recordings of live and studio work to the "Snakey Wake" played for Phillip Lithman. They also issued a quarterly newsletter as well as a number of updated versions of "Santa Dog".

God In Three Persons spawned a 20 minute 3" CD single "Holy Kiss Of Flesh" as well as "Doubleshot" which was also released as a single. There were plans at one stage to tour the project in operatic form and an overture was written. However, plans were abandoned in favour of another, more ambitious live project.

Footnotes
1. Snakefinger to *Sonics* Nov/Dec 1986.
2. Ralph Records press release.
3. Ralph Records Press release.
4. Hardy Fox to *Sonics* Nov/Dec 1986
5. Ibid.
6. *New Musical Express*, 1st November 1986.
7. *Melody Maker*, 1st November 1986.
8. Edwin Pouncey. Interview with Author. January 1993.
9. J.Raul Brody. Interview with Author. October 1992.
10. Hardy Fox.
11. Edwin Pouncey. Interview with Author. January 1993.
12. Homer Flynn to *Music and Sound Output*, 1988
13. Hardy Fox to *Music and Sound Output*, 1988
14. Ibid.
15. Ibid.

SUBTLE REVIEW
© MATT HOWARTH
I WAS IMPOSSIBLY DETAINED.. WHAT DID I MISS SO FAR?
OH, IT'S UNMISTAKENLY ANOTHER ALBUM BY THE RESIDENTS... STARS & HANK FOREVER$. POSSIBLY THEIR STRANGEST MUSICAL ESCAPADE YET. LOYAL BUT CAREFULLY MUTATED COVER SONGS BY
HANK WILLIAMS
AND JOHN PHILIP SOUSA
AMONG THE HANK WILLIAMS SONGS ARE "HEY GOOD LOOKIN'" AND "RAMBLIN' MAN", FEATURING A DEEPLY KALEIDOPHONIC SOUND WITH ELECTRO DRAWL VOCALS, WHISTLING HORNS, SLOW TWANG PEDAL STEEL GUITAR, SPECTRAL HARMONIES, AND AN OVERALL GUMBY WAGON TRAIN MOOD TO IT.
THOSE RESIDENTS ARE WAY TOO COOL.
THE USE OF APPLAUSE ON THE SOUSASIDE IMPRESSIVELY SETS THE SONIC SCENARIO OF A MARCHING BAND OF RESIDENTS DANCING AROUND A FOOTBALL STADIUM, PERFORMING BUZZING CLOCKWORK COVERS OF INSTANTLY RECOGNIZABLE SOUSA CLASSICS.
A BRILLIANT AND EXCESSIVE CASE OF SILLY WEIRDNESS... ASCENDING KEYBOARDS LIKE ACCORDION ROLLS, TINY ACOUSTICAL GUITARS, MAMBO RHYTHM MACHINES, WHINY SYNTH HORNS, FLUTELIKE PIANO, THE GAZEBO SOUND of WHEEZING PIPE ORGANS, AMPHIBIOUS SYNTHESIZER PINGS AND WHIRS... JUST HILARIOUS!
$ THE AMERICAN COMPOSER SERIES, VOLUME 2 — ON RALPH RECORDS. CONTACT: 109 MINNA, BOX 391, SAN FRANCISCO, CA. 94105

CUBE E

"This show was probably one of The Residents better business decisions and the reason it was such a good business decision was because they put so much energy into merchandising. What we discovered in terms of trying to create touring performances these days is that it may or not make great art but it makes lousy business...

What happened with The Residents when they toured (Cube E) they did about seventy five to eighty performances of the show and, as far as the actual tour went, they probably showed a profit of, oh...maybe four or five thousand dollars. But the merchandising was gangbusters! Ultimately what it amounts to...is the show becomes a promotional device for a T-shirt selling business."[1]

Homer Flynn

Unlike the Mole Show and the 13th Anniversary Show, the *Cube E* tour of 1988-90 was not conceived as one long performance piece. It came together slowly.

The Residents discovered an authentic book of cowboy poems and songs. Intrigued, they researched further and slowly constructed a short suite of songs around the theme of the old "Wild West" in their newly installed MIDI recording studio. This became "Buckeroo Blues" which was first heard by fan club members when released on CD (UWEB 003) – which also contained the "Overture" for the abandoned *God In Three Persons* opera.

"Buckeroo Blues" was premiered at a party for Boudisque (Torso) Records (their European label) in Amsterdam on November 18th, 1987, when The Residents performed the track sitting at a table. It was subsequently performed live on German TV for the programme *Tele 5* in April, 1988. The half-hour performance was fleshed out with a live version of Hank Williams' "Jambalaya" and Elvis Presley's "Burning Love". Filmed in front of a live audience and a static camera, The Residents presented an early version of the choreography for the "Buckeroo Blues" segment of the *Cube E* show dressed in black cowboy suits.

With the vague idea of constructing a new touring performance piece around a thematic history of American music, a second piece slowly developed around the contribution of black music – jazz and blues – to American music and this became "Black Barry". These two suites were performed live at New York's Lincoln Centre in July, 1989.

However, The Residents encountered great difficulties in trying to decide what the third and concluding suite of music was to be. How to complete the concept of the history of American music in three easy parts. In an attempt to resolve this dilemma they rented a motel room for two nights and spent the entire forty-eight hours brainstorming.

After much heated discussion one came up with an idea that embodied everything that was American popular music – a medley of Elvis Presley songs performed by an Elvis imitator. The other Residents violently disagreed and more importantly, did not think that they would be able to pull it off in live performance. They were, however, slowly won around, and when they checked out of the motel, a medley of Elvis songs performed by a grandfather Elvis imitator as the third part of the show had been agreed upon.

It was now a question of working out which Elvis songs, designing costumes, working out choreography and building up the theatrics of the entire performance. Unlike their previous two tours *Cube-E* was not to be a "concept" or "concert" performance but a theatrical piece with musical accompaniment. The Lead Singer would not simply sing songs but, in conjunction with two dancers, would "act out" each piece. He would dance, perform, and like Elvis before him, mop his brow with silk scarves and throw them out into the audience. This was worked out by the Singer in conjunction with choreographers – Sarah McLennen and Carol Lemaitre. It was a very interactive process. "Watching (him) move and then taking that and exaggerating it or suggesting new things or different things or choreography."…. "It was a real exchange of ideas between all of us. Generally we were given an idea of what was going to happen and what the props and what the set is and we would fill in the blanks."[2]

The finished choreography was designed to be "…very focussed and slow moving at the beginning, picked up a little and then kind of blew it out at the end so that the audience could get an emotional release at the end…"[3] McLennan and Lemaitre also danced on the tour and found working with The Residents highly stimulating. Carol Lemaitre:

"A typical dancer will rehearse for six months and perform once or twice. With this group you can rehearse for two weeks and perform a hundred times. It's a great opportunity to get to do the same show over and over and over and find much more depth in it. And that to me is the most exciting thing about working with The Residents, in that things change and grow and evolve in performance and they're very open to that and a show develops on stage as opposed to developing in rehearsal."[4]

As with the Mole Show, The Residents did not want to have typical "rock" lighting. It had to be theatrical and supportive to the performance. To undertake this task they turned to stage lighting expert Chris McGregor. McGregor had seen the 13th Anniversary show and had been appalled by the minimal lighting and knew he could do better. With The Residents blessing he set out to prove it.

The theatrical nature of *Cube-E* meant that the three pieces would be acted out against various coloured backdrops upon which different back projections could be made to visually complement and enhance the performance. In order to emphasise the actions of the performers, a decision was made to use ultra-violet black light.

Ultra-violet black light is created by placing filters over fluorescent tubes which filter out colour. Therefore the only light emitted is ultra-violet black light and any material responsive to this type of light will glow as if light is coming from within them. Non-responsive material would not respond at all and it creates what McGregor describes as a "very powerful, intense effect". To achieve this strong visual effect for *Cube-E* a dozen huge powerful factory sodium vapour and mercury lighting units were laid in front of the stage like footlights and covered with very intense filters. This meant that the performers could go anywhere and the light sensitive materials on their costumes would pick up the ultra-violet light.

The costumes for the three parts of the performance were designed and manufactured to enhance this effect. For example, in the "Buckeroo Blues" sequence the Lead Resident and the two dancers wore totally black costumes with huge black ten gallon hats. Red light sensitive material was stitched onto the chest and the Lead Resident also had huge white lips on the Beefheart-ish Trout

Masks each performer wore. The final touch was the use of two pen lights supported by glasses to serve as white glowing eyes.

McGregor worked closely with The Residents to maximise the dynamics offered by this creative use of lighting and tweaked the show during performances to accommodate local conditions as well as adding new effects to enhance the performance. For example, when a cinema screen proved unresponsive to black light it was discovered that the Elvis portion of the show worked much better with total darkness behind the performers rather than back projections. A black curtain was incorporated into the show to obtain this effect. "It was like creating a piece of art and then watching it metamorphasise over the two and a half year period we toured", McGregor remembers.

The music for Cube E was performed by three musicians at the back of the stage off to the right. For "Buckeroo Blues" some of the music was sequenced direct from the computer, except for the opening sax break and the Lead Resident's vocals. The same applied to "Black Barry" although some parts were played live to add some human timing, a human feeling to it. All of the music on the third part – "The Baby King" – was played live by the musicians using computer generated samples.

The first fully integrated three part performance of *Cube E* took place in San Francisco at the Cowell Theatre on September 21st, 1989 and received a standing ovation. In total, The Residents played six sell-out shows in four days inside the 440 seater theatre before heading off on a European tour where they received equally enthusiastic responses from sell-out crowds.

One of the strongest features of *Cube-E* was that it did not require any pre-knowledge of The Residents, their music or their past. Even the eyeball albatross was abandoned in favour of newly designed cubist eyeballs (Cube-Es) that only made a brief appearance after the show. Apparently, The Residents were so fed up with the Tuxedo and eyeball association that they specified in the contract for each concert performance that they would not wear them. *Cube-E* was a fully integrated theatrical performance piece that anybody could come, see, understand and enjoy. The music was not grating, unusual or weird but melodic and very easy on the ear – "that's right: The Residents music is now *accessible*"[5] – a soundtrack to support a cinematic performance.

And what a performance! After a fanfare from a ghetto blaster playing the 20th Century Fox theme the curtain would part to reveal three cowboys in huge ten gallon hats sitting around a glowing red campfire against a blue backdrop studded with white stars. The music would commence and one cowboy would stand and bowleggedly sing "From the Plains to Mexico" to his two companions and the audience. More songs would follow as well as Cowboy dancing, a knife fight and the death and burial of "Old Red".

The second part – "Black Barry" – saw the main three protagonists dressed in reflective white shirts and black bodystockings. The music is very powerful and the theme suggests that black America sold its music to win acceptance. It culminates with the dramatic appearance of the huge box-headed "Black Barry" figure suggesting the rising up of black Americans from slavery.

The climax of *Cube E* was of course Elvis. Once the audience had returned from the interval, they would hear "Thus Spake Zarathustra", the trademark music Elvis used before taking the stage for his Las Vegas shows. The curtain would part to reveal an old Elvis imitator asleep in a chair with his two woodentop grandchildren – Shorty and Shirley – sitting on his lap. Waking up he would relate the story of "The Baby King" – Elvis – to them. "I used to pretend that I was kind of part of it... I'll show you guys a bit if you like... let's see if I can remember how it goes..." He would then stand up, and garbed in a fantastic light reactive costume and striking black and white face make-up, launch himself into "Don't be Cruel," "Devil In Disguise," "Burning Love," "Teddy Bear" and other seminal Elvis Presley songs delivered in typically Residential style.

This part of *Cube-E* is stunning, especially when the two dancers portray Las Vegas showgirls (with red light reflective tits 'n' ass). They then form their bodies into a heart of roses and Elvis dons a huge stomach and belt to signify his decline. The climax of the entire performance comes when he is symbolically "killed" by blasts of sampled music from The Beatles and The Rolling Stones – the English Invasion. This was a typically Residential touch and the perfect way of bringing the performance to a close. There were no encores.

Taken as a whole, the performance was breathtaking and marked a second high watermark of The Residents' career. *Cube-E* combines elements of music, theatre and performance into a compelling audio and visual spectacle. Audience reaction, especially in Europe was fantastic. Lighting man Chris McGregor:

"...you pull into Athens and it's like you're with The Beatles. All of a sudden there's a riot on the street in front of the venue because they could not sell enough tickets and they're rocking police cars around. The band had to be covered up and run the gauntlet to the backstage entrance."[6]

A Resident recalls another anecdote:

"In Berlin we got a standing ovation that lasted longer than the show. We were already completely broken down... we were wandering around in the crowd drinking beer and they were still applauding."[7]

In Bologna the Italian promoter was unclear about the concept. He announced that there would be two intervals rather than one. At the end of the show The Residents left the stage and prepared for the curtain call. When they took to the stage, the lights were up and the auditorium virtually empty. "Everybody was out in the lobby smoking cigarettes and drinking cappucchino going 'How are they going to top that?'"[8]

Despite the spectacular nature of the show, unlike the Mole Show, there were no major financial problems. There was tight financial control over every aspect of the tour from travel arrangements to all matters of merchandising. (There were even specially produced *Cube-E* plastic bags for fans to take their goodies home in). There were a few minor quirks. The computer system containing all the sequenced music "crashed" in New York, but manager and computer expert Rich Shupe was on hand to sort it out. On a train between Italy and Germany a thief got into one of The Residents' compartments and stole a substantial amount of money from his money belt. The Resident was unphased, "It's only money. It could have been something important." When The Residents played Tel Aviv, in Israel, they faxed ahead their lighting requirements, flew in, did the show and then flew out five hours later. Members of the Israeli army prepared the theatre for the performance.

Back in America, The Residents played another string of sold-out shows at the Cowell Theatre in San Francisco culminating in a New Year's Eve performance where each member of the audience received a free CD – "For Elsie", The Residents interpreting Beethoven! This was also released as a one sided collector's LP, standing without doubt head and shoulders above The Residents interpretations of the music of George Gershwin and Sousa. It takes one melodic and recognisable piece and gives it several different interpretations. All different. All excellent.

On the stroke of midnight The Residents played the first and last *Cube-E* encore with a "version" of "Auld Lang Syne" and the first ever live version of "Santa Dog". In the new year they moved onto the Florence Gould Hall, New York for several shows and a slot on David Sanborn's prestigious "Night Music" on 14th January, 1990. The Residents had agreed to appear on "Night Music" and showcase a couple of tracks from *Cube-E*. However, when Chris McGregor went into the studio with a long list of their lighting requirements, a disagreement ensued. The producers wanted The Residents to simply play like any other band without any theatrical presentation. The Residents, however, were not any band. As McGregor argued:

> "The Who or Genesis, with all of their huge systems, their lights and their explosions... could go into a studio and still make beautiful music and still please everybody, in fact people would be thrilled to see that happen. But The Residents, so much of the visual is the show. You can't take that away from The Residents, it's not all about music – which is what it is with Genesis or The Who, a band, a rock band – here we're dealing with artists who have a whole vision of how the show is presented."[9]

The producers and Sanborn relented after seeing one of the New York performances of *Cube-E*. They saw how the presentation was the performance. However, when it came to arranging the lighting of the two numbers to be performed, there was still "much butting of heads" with the Union stagehands. Only when the lighting director Phil Hyams arrived, – an "old New York cigar smoking, raspy character" – did things change. He was very understanding and interested in The Residents creative use of lighting. He barked out orders and got the ball rolling. What the audience got to see was a fantastic version of "From the Plains To Mexico" and a cover version of "Teddy Bear" that was "so aggressive they got more viewer mail than any other act... either extremely appreciative or extremely unappreciative."[10] The Residents also got to "Twist" with the late Conway Twitty.

Unfortunately, these two numbers were the only part of *Cube-E* to be filmed. (Apart from the embryonic German TV footage). Although *Cube-E* was performed around 80 times, not a single performance was commercially filmed. This was a shame as *Cube-E* was a truly groundbreaking show, and considering The Residents fascination with archiving their long career, well worth preserving. Apparently there were some interested parties but no-one came up with the right financial package to make it happen. The Residents toyed with financing it themselves but finally abandoned the idea as they were of the opinion that:

> "If something was going to be filmed it would not be *Cube E* because it was something that ultimately had to be experienced live for it to carry across."[11]

Cube-E was so successful that it ended up touring twice. In 1990 more dates were played in Europe and America. This time, however, there was a mixed response. Chris McGregor:

> "In Europe there were big audiences, there were enthusiastic audiences, they were responsive and interested in the thing The Residents were doing. The range of audiences was phenomenal; everything from the expectant punks in black leather to old couples, to people wearing suits to hippies, a rich broad range.
>
> Here (America) it was very much your college music audience, who, I think, it might have been a little artsy for them. Some of

them were very responsive, but most of them were into REM or the latest thing in the hit parade. It's scary to think someone as avant-garde and revolutionary as The Residents are relegated to old phogey status by guys waiting for the next Peter Gabriel album."[12]

The final American dates were dogged with misfortune. One Cleveland promoter declared himself bankrupt as The Residents stepped out on the stage and, as he was promoting the next concert, they would be in effect be playing for free as no-one was there to pay them. The performance was cancelled. The last performance of *Cube-E* took place in New York in November, 1990. A speaker cabinet fell from the stage and crashed into a fortunately unoccupied seat in the front row and a small fire broke out on stage. It was quickly extinguished. The Residents, detecting that The Mark Of The Mole Tour might be coming back to haunt them, flew back to San Francisco forthwith.

Footnotes
1. Homer Flynn at The Museum Of Modern Art. New York. 19th October 1992.
2. Sarah Mclennen and Carol Lemaitre. Interview with Author. October 1992.
3. Ibid.
4. Carol Lemaitre. Interview with Author, October 1992.
5. Barry Walters: *San Francisco Examiner*, Sept 22, 1989.
6. Chris McGregor. Interview with Author. October 1992.
7. A Resident. Interview with Author. October 1992.
8. J.Raul Brody. Interview with Author, October 1992.
9. Chris McGregor. Interview with Author. October 1992.
10. Rich Shupe. Interview with Author. October 1992.
11. Chris McGregor. Interview with Author. October 1992.
12. Ibid.

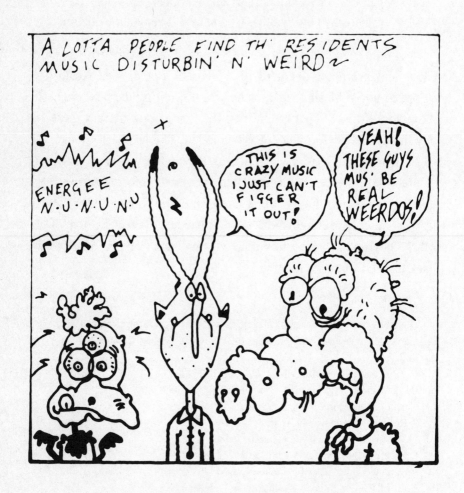

Who the hell are The Residents...? 5

Cartoon by Savage Pencil from Rock and Roll Zoo.

WELCOME TO THE FREAK SHOW

"Hurry! Hurry! Hurry! Step right up and you will see on display a collection of some of the strangest specimens ever gathered together – both live and preserved."[1]

From the lyrics to Freak Show

To coincide with the *Cube-E* tour, The Residents had released *The King and Eye* in 1989, which was an entire LP of cover versions of Elvis songs. It was a fairly uninspired affair and this may have something to do with the fact that it was recorded in a commercial studio rather than their own. Booking themselves into Different Fur studios in San Francisco, The Residents wanted to see what it was like working against the clock with a finite amount of expensive studio time. They found out. The songs are bland, flat and totally lack sparkle. The results sound rushed. The cover art – depicting a crucified skeletal Elvis – has more bite.

In fact, *The King and Eye* saw a new development in the art department. Poreknowgraphics would still devise the cover art and images but the packaging was handed over to graphic designer Rex Ray. Ray was not the first to assist The Residents with their packaging, for five years in the early '80s Helen Hall was the art director at Ralph records. Rex Ray, incidentally, handled all of the

UWEB fan club CD cover art in his very personalised distinct style. As he didn't have to worry about the "direct sales impact", he could do as he pleased. For the record, Rex used to work part time packaging mail order at Ralph Records whilst studying Video and Conceptual Performance Arts at the San Francisco Art Institute. Rex also has the accolade of telling me the most amusing Residents' anecdote. Unfortunately, for reasons best left muddy, it cannot be related within these pages.

Ironically, these Elvis covers sound much better in live performance as demonstrated on the CD release of the Cube-E show *Live in Holland*. Raw, rougher and obviously live. Perhaps, the studio created *The King and Eye* was simply a template for the live show.

Of course, riding on the back of Cube-E this somewhat bland album sold tremendously well. "Don't be Cruel" was released as a single and The Residents created a breathtaking computer generated video – lots of disfigured Elvis's and garishly coloured dollar bills – to promote it. It even made MTV.

Ironically, around this time The Residents were receiving heavy rotation on MTV although it was not one of their videos being shown. "Slow Bob in the Lower Dimensions" was a five minute pilot for a new animated series of MTV shorts by San Francisco-based director Henry Selick who was responsible for animating a large number of the famous MTV logo identification pieces. This led to them scoring the five episodes of *The Adventures of Thomas and Nordo* aired on MTV in 1992. The Residents hoped that this would be the start of a new trend and see them receiving more commissions for film and TV soundtrack work like that which they had already produced for Pee Wee Herman's playhouse.

In the meantime they continued to produce music, and in 1991 released *Freak Show*. As the title suggests this was a concept album based on the freak shows that had once toured America. They, no doubt, drew inspiration from the considerable amount of literature available on this subject, especially *Freak Show* by Robert Boydan (University of Chicago Press), *Freaks* by Daniel P.Mannix (ReSearch) and *Human Oddities* by Martin Monestier (Citadel). They were also possibly inspired by the extraordinary 1932 movie *Freaks* that controversially documented a group of disfigured and malformed performers as real people with intellect and feelings rather than simply side-show attractions.

Considered by many as musical freaks themselves (and playing up to it) it was a logical conclusion of Residential musical exploration. They did the concept justice with sly carnivalesque songs about a troupe of Resident-created freaks like "Benny the Bouncing Bump", "Wanda the Worm Woman" and "Harry The Head". The record again featured the talents of Laurie Amat whose freakish vocal qualities were perfectly suited to the project. *Freak Show* was recorded in The Residents own studio on a computerised MIDI system with the assistance of Tony Janssen who had been responsible for the excellent sound on the Cube E tour and CD release, and whose ideas strongly influenced the sound of the finished music.

The concept of *Freak Show* was not confined to music alone and over the next couple of years was to spawn a whole host of other products in different media. Firstly, there was the absolutely fantastic promotional video for the single "Harry the Head". This promo was created by computer graphic genius Jim Ludtke on an Apple Macintosh computer and was visually stunning. So much so that it began to be used by Apple to demonstrate the graphic versatility of their computers.

Then there was the *Freak Show* comic. Published by Dark Horse Comics in 1992 this was a bold and imaginative step, featuring eight different artists visually interpreting a track from the LP. The artists featured were, Brian Bolland, John Bolton, Matt Howarth, Dave McKean, Richard Sala, Savage Pencil, Les Dorscheid and Pore Know Graphics himself. Each contributed his own distinctive graphic style to portray an individual and unique vision of one of the Freaks on show.

The comic was lavishly produced and was a wonderful promotional tool, not only for the *Freak Show* LP, but also served to introduce The Residents and their music to an entirely different market. Two pages were also devoted exclusively to the sale of Residential product like watches, eyeball ear rings and a limited edition silkscreen portfolio of *Freak Show* comic art. Plans were made to release the comic in hard back form sometime in 1993 with a fifteen minute "sampler" CD – *Blowoff* – of instrumental Residential *Freak Show* music as well as what sounds like an out-take from the album.

On 15th November 1991, The Residents were hired for a twenty minute performance by computer giant NEC. The performance took place in the Fairmont Hotel, San Jose in front of an invited audience of computer software experts. The Residents, assisted by Laurie Amat, featured material from *Freak Show*. The concert was filmed and edited live to demonstrate the effectiveness of a new video deck and editing equipment. A six minute mix of this show was subsequently used for demonstration purposes by Apple Computers on CD-ROM and limited distribution VHS video.

Always interested in new media, in 1991 The Cryptic Corporation struck a deal with the Voyager Company that was active in the visionary area of media known as "electronic interactive publishing". The first fruit of this partnership was the release in early 1992 of a Residents laserdisc entitled *Twenty Twisted Questions*. A laserdisc is basically a 12" record that holds images instead of music inside its grooves. The Residents' half-hour laserdisc contained most of the old promotional films like "Land of 1,000 Dances," and "It's a Man's World" as well as an exhaustive interactive Residents discography that allowed the viewer to view album covers and hear a thirty second "sample" of music from each release. The viewer could also "freeze frame" and read the short biographical details about the release.

If this was The Residents setting their stall out in what will eventually become an industry standard format (especially the way music has become synonomous with promotional video these days) the next Voyager project took them to the cutting edge of new technology; the *Freak Show* CD-ROM.

Like the "Harry The Head" video this was completely designed by computer artist Jim Ludtke. Basically, it was not just computer generated promo clips to accompany the LP, but a totally interactive package where the viewer/player could poke around inside the *Freak Show* circus tent, the performers' caravans (The Residents' one was a huge eyeball) and command each freak (including The Residents) to perform. The animation of these sequences is truly breathtaking and defies description. I personally, saw a demonstration of this before completion and it was like nothing I have ever seen, combining top notch animation, comic book like graphics with swooping cinematic technique. As to whether it will sell or point the way ahead is another matter entirely, but it has already turned heads inside the computer graphics industry. Again, it has been shown as a demonstration piece. Rich Shupe explains that, "The Residents create ideas... and Jim goes to town with the art."[2] The Residents worked very closely with Ludtke speaking to him 3 or 4 times a day as well as meeting him once or twice a week to look at his designs and make suggestions. It was a very interactive process.

The finished product certainly does the *Freak Show* concept justice. It is explorative and interactive. You can not only enter the Freak Show tent and get the freaks to perform for you. Homer Flynn:

> "There's a little sign that says "Keep Out". Well, of course, any adventurous person will not pay any attention to that... when you get to the backstage area you can then go inside all these trailers and explore the personal environment of each one of these freaks and what we're doing is juxtaposing the superficial facade. That's out here in the tent, we're comparing that to the artefacts of the real person that we have on the inside."[3]

No doubt the Residential hard core fans will be scrambling out to buy CD-ROM players when it is released at the end of 1993.

1992 had marked twenty years of Resident activity since the release of "Santa Dog" in 1972. To celebrate this anniversary there were a series of low key events. On 19th October, Homer Flynn gave a talk entitled "Hissing and Kissing the Wind" at the New York Museum of Modern Art that examined the twenty years of activity as well as showing original 16mm films of "Land of 1,000 Dances", "Hello Skinny" and the "One Minute Movies" and premiering work in progress from the forthcoming *Freak Show* CD-ROM. There was also concurrent exhibition of Residential performance artefacts at The Kitchen with specially composed accompanying music.

The year was supposed to end in spectacular style with a fan convention and a Residents live performance on the 26th December 1992 (Boxing day) at the Cowell Theatre, San Francisco. However, this was cancelled due to the amount of time The Residents were spending working on the CD-ROM project.

There was, of course, a special 20th Anniversary release. Fighting off the temptation to release a repackaged compilation of their greatest hits they chose instead to mix them all up in the computer and match various backing tracks with various vocals, splice tracks together, re-record some parts, and generally create something new out of their old material. Working again with Tony Janssen it took a year to record. The completed package was entitled *Our Finest Flowers* and was released at the tail end of 1992.

Probably the most significant part of this collection was that it came out on Ralph Records, which The Residents had recovered from Tom Timony in 1991 after their five year agreement with him to use the name had expired. It is an interesting and satisfying release although somewhat contrived. Those unfamiliar with the vast Residents back catalogue will probably not be able to recognise the complex interwoven strands and motifs. However, it was a vast improvement on *Ten Years in Twenty Minutes* which had been released in 1982 that celebrated their first ten years of recording activity. Here snatches of every single Residents song were stuck together to form one long continuous "suite" of music.

In 1993 The Residents decided to close down their fan club UWEB. This was due in large part to the creation of Ralph America – a mail order operation that was established to market their back catalogue, sell off archives like original artwork, copies of rare releases to mark twenty years of existence, and more esoteric items like fake human eyeballs and an amazing assortment of eyeball jewellery. A similar operation – Euro Ralph – was established in Europe.

As for the next twenty years there were plans to transform one of their greatest works – *Eskimo* – into an opera. A synopsis was drawn up, complete with computer generated stage diagrams. Due to the logistical problems of putting it on, the *Eskimo* opera would not tour, but would only play in several locations worldwide – Berlin, Amsterdam, London, San Francisco and New York. Presentations were made to the Amsterdam Opera House and an interested party in Germany with a view to obtaining the necessary $150,000 seed financing. However, nothing came of these negotiations.

Since then there have been fruitful negotiations with a Czechoslovakian theatre group with a view to a collaboration on an entirely new live concept piece. What it is to be about is a tightly guarded secret but sources reveal that it will be visually and musically unlike anything they have ever produced before. More mainstream. If the financing works out it is likely to be premiered in 1995. Of course, until then The Residents have a number of projects to keep themselves busy. They have been commissioned to produce the music for a ten hour nature series which will occupy them in the latter part of 1993 and early 1994. This is a project they are very excited about and something they see occupying a larger proportion of their time in the future. They have just put the finishing touches to a new EP and there are also plans to record new material for an album in 1994.

Footnotes
1. Lyrics from "Everyone Come to the Freak Show". From *Freak Show* LP, 1990.
2. Rich Shupe. Interview with Author, October 1992.
3. Homer Flynn. Museum of Modern Art, October 1992.

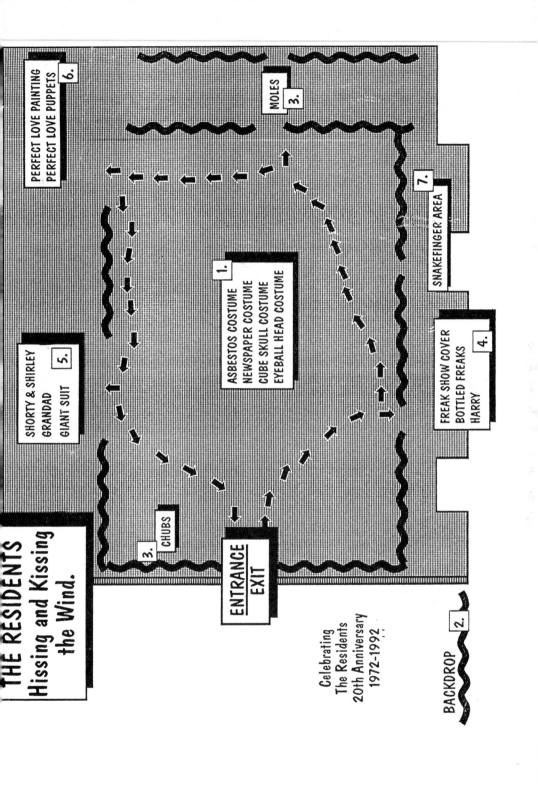

THE RESIDENTS
Hissing and Kissing the Wind.

PERFECT LOVE PAINTING
PERFECT LOVE PUPPETS
6.

MOLES
3.

7.
SNAKEFINGER AREA

1.
ASBESTOS COSTUME
NEWSPAPER COSTUME
CUBE SKULL COSTUME
EYEBALL HEAD COSTUME

SHORTY & SHIRLEY
GRANDAD
GIANT SUIT
5.

FREAK SHOW COVER
BOTTLED FREAKS
HARRY
4.

3.
CHUBS

ENTRANCE
EXIT

Celebrating
The Residents
20th Anniversary
1972-1992

BACKDROP
2.

Hissing And Kissing The Wind: Some Aging Artifacts in Formal Installation

Opening reception: Wednesday, October 14, 1992 6pm
Thursday, October 15 - Friday November 6, 1992 Mondays - Fridays 12 - 6pm

The Residents have been heralded as among the "inventors" of music video. Their Vileness Fats project, begun in 1972, was the first audio/visual concept project shot in video for non-theatrical distribution. Since then, the ensemble has created some of the most original bodies of work in music video, as well as numerous live performance events. Famed for their quirky and powerful imagery, these eyeball-headed performers have maintained complete anonymity during their twenty-year career. This installation includes many of props, costumes, and scenic elements used by The Residents.

The Artifacts:

1. Selected Costumes: Asbestos Costume (1977); Newspaper Costume (1972); Cube Skull Costume (1989); Eyeball Head Costume (1979)

The Mole Show, The Residents' first touring performance, included the use of 22 backdrops in the performance, the moles, ugly but sweet underground workers, after being driven from their home by a natural disaster migrate to a country of technologically sophisticated but superficial beings who try to exploit their labor (Chubs). The Chubs eventually create a machine which will replace the moles' labor, and a war is begun. The performance ends in unresolved conflict. (2 & 3.)

2. Mole Show backdrops: Eleven canvas backdrops, each 15 feet high and 10 feet wide, used in the Mole Show performance (1982 - 1983)

3. Moles and Chubs: Canvas props represent characters used in The Mole Show performance (1982 - 1983)

Freak Show is an ongoing project of The Residents with three segments to date, a music album, a performance, and a graphic novel. The Residents are currently developing a Freak Show CD ROM. Freak Show reveals the freakishness of the normal and the normality of the freak. Harry, King of the freaks, is also the star of a music video.

4. Scenic elements from Freak Show (1990 - present) Freak Show Cover: painting on canvas (6 feet x 6 feet); Bottled Freaks:100 bottles and jars containing doll parts; toys, and other media. Harry, King of the Bottled Freaks

Cube E. consists of the tale of Elvis, told by Grandad, an aging Elvis impersonator, to Shorty and Shirley. Weaving a tale of cowboys, gospel music, and American history, Grandad depicts Elvis as long lost king. In the final act of Cube E, Cubehead, a gospel singer arises as an omnipotent figure.

5. Scenic elements from Cube E. performance (1989 - 1990); Grandad Costume; Shorty and Shirley (puppets) on Grandad's Chair; Giant Cube Head Costume

6. Perfect Love: Fuzzy version of Perfect Love music video accompanied by scenic elements from the video (1980).

7. Snakefinger Area. Artifacts from The Residents' late great guitarist, Snakefinger (1949 - 1987). Snakefinger's coat, boots, and photograph; Poster, given to him by The Residents, from a Bobby "Blue" Bland Concert.

Stephen Gallagher	Exhibition Curator
Homer Flynn	Business Manager for The Residents
Stephen Rueff	Lighting Design
Sue Hamburger	Technical Director
Cat Domiano, Michael McLaughlin, and Isaac Taylor	Installation Crew
Omar Khalid	Production Intern
Michele Rosenshein	Program Coordinator

Special thanks to Susan Glass/Materials for the Arts, Barbara London/MoMA, George Alonzo/Hindsgaul, Goldsmith, Inc., Callender Trucking, Cryptic Corp., the staff of The Kitchen, Lee and Isabelle.

Please wad this paper up and throw it on the floor when you are finished

THE OBSCURITY CONTINUES...

Ultimately, part of the joy of appreciating The Residents mythology is to be swept along with their attempts to recreate themselves in various guises, without perhaps looking too deeply into their true identities. For this reason, I reiterate that I have purposefully been evasive as to who The Residents are, or how many make up their number – as this is so central to their mythology I decided that this book should at least in part reflect and respect their attempts to remain anonymous.

I have taken the view that the question of what The Residents' body of work over the last 20 years represents, is ultimately a more important and intriguing a question. In any event, merely sustaining a career for that length of time in an industry as fickle as the music business is some achievement. A vast majority of bands find it difficult to satisfy the public's craving for "something new" beyond the first three LP syndrome, especially if they have not broken through into wide enough acceptance to justify reinvestment by their record company. Many bands simply hit a peak early on and then fade away. Others splinter into factions, record solo projects and eventually reform for one last money making tour. Some are one hit wonders. Even more tend to live on in CD reissued back catalogues and journalists "whatever happened to...." columns.

All this of course supposes that The Residents can be compared in some ways to other bands. In a lot of ways The Residents are unique. They have always done everything on their terms, and certainly at times it would be difficult compare their music to that of any other band. However, at times their discordant musical structure has links in both classical avant-garde and jazz worlds and with early Captain Beefheart. Their obsessive secrecy and attempts to rewrite their own history is somewhat akin to Kraftwerk, and their stoically independently minded record and label distribution bares more than a passing resemblance to Frank Zappa's position over his vast output. Certainly The Residents fondness for cover versions is common place in the rock business.

However, the number of bands that have remained together unscathed through two decades is rare. Even the Rolling Stones and the Grateful Dead have lost the odd member over the years. Very few groups are still going strong and continue to record new material. There are now all too many bands who engage in million dollar tours that lean heavily upon an impressive back catalogue which is guaranteed to hit the right chord with audiences whatever their age level or familiarity. Whenever Keith Richards cranks up his guitar to play "Satisfaction" he does so to howls of instant recognition.

We are at a time where the music industry values its fortysomething leathery faced treasures. They are in vogue like never before and remain industry best sellers, often with the help of an MTV unplugged show here or there.

The Residents differ from what I may loosely term their contemporaries. In the first place they have never shifted enough units. Being fiercely independent about their releases on a musical and business level has ensured that they have never had any recognisable hit singles or Billboard top 100 LP's. Their obsessive insistence on anonymity has guarateed that even their distinctive image has not crept into the collective consciousness. They remain a cultish acquired taste – a taste that even after 20 years can sometimes seem bitter and unpalatable. In some ways that is something to be thankful for. The Residents can still intrigue because they don't have the comfort of relying upon a few old hits and the treadmill of nostaligic live perfomances to remind people that they are still around – after all we have groups like The Beach Boys or The Kinks to remind us of that sorry state. Without the excessive baggage of "hits", The Residents can continue to move forward with confidence.

However, everyone's past catches up with them sooner or later. Whether they like it or not, to some, The Residents are a nostalgic reminder of better days in the independent sector when people could more easily record, market their own records, run their own labels. A bygone age when producing something arresting and challenging seemed possible without buckling under the strain of commercial pressures. If pushed, even The Residents might have to admit the fact that this is an increasingly difficult aim to achieve. However, The Residents try not to wallow in the romanticism of the past and have no truck with those (maybe myself included) who listen to their old records from the '70s and might be tempted to rely on how avant-garde they were in the good old days.

The Residents move onwards, ever widening their artistic window on the world. After 21 years they are at the stage of development where they now conceive fully integrated projects rather than songs. These days music is only a part of the product line The Residents wish to sell. They are heavily involved in all areas of visual interactive media. *Freak Show* is part of a trend for them. It was an LP, comic, interactive CD-Rom, limited edition art prints and a whole host of paraphernalia.

This is a "think tank" that still generates a frightening amount of ideas. Only a lack of financial resources stops them from realising the more ambitious of them. They are no longer simply looking to release music and tour. They have done that. They are always on the look out for new areas for venting their artistic spleens. They are looking to stage operas and musicals with huge sets and modern concepts. They want to make a full length feature film to do their visual sense justice. They are keen to get more involved with radical new developments in computer graphics, computer games and are seriously considering a chain of Resident theme shops. Who knows there may even be plans for a Disneyesque 'Residentsland'. As to whether their ideas come to fruition or remain pie-in-the-sky is yet to be seen. However, The Residents have enough provisions to sustain their journey into the next 21 years and you can be sure that they will be inspired with the surreal sense of the ridiculous that has been with them ever since they started.

All this contrives not only to make their position unique but also difficult to sum up their achievements. Certainly, they have spawned very few imitators. Their approach to music has been so eccentric at times that it would be difficult to imagine people trying to recreate what they do. Similarly, few could be bothered with keeping up such a wall of secrecy – and anyway most people's egos would probably be unsatisfied with type of anonymity they have insisited on. However, ultimately they may have one distinct advantage over their contemporaries – plastic eyeballs don't wrinkle with age!

Who the hell are The Residents...? 6
Cartoon by Savage Pencil from Rock and Roll zoo.

DISCOGRAPHY

The complete Residents discography is absolutely huge. As well as official releases there are also a large number of limited editions, collectors items, coloured vinyls, cassettes, re-releases, picture discs, singles, radio specials, flexi discs, Anniversary Commemorative issues, fan club only CD's etc. etc. etc! The majority of these items – especially originals from the period 1972-78 – are highly collectable and no longer readily availiable in their original format. Fortunately, the American company East Side Digital and Torso in Europe have undertaken an exhaustive CD reissue of The Residents back catalogue and thankfully included are most of the rare tracks from singles/EP's as bonus tracks. The following discography only lists these CD releases as they are easy to obtain. Residential masochists should seek out Ralph America's extensive discography. *Uncle Willies Highly Opinionated Guide to The Residents* also contains an exhaustive discography.

For the record the Schwump single has, and never will be, re-issued in any form whatsoever. It will pass into infinity as a limited edition of 200.

MEET THE RESIDENTS (Torso CD 416)
Boots, Numb Erone, Guylum Bardot, Breath and Length, Consuelo's Departure, Smelly Tongues, Rest Aria, Skratz, Spotted Pinto Bean.
Bonus Tracks: Santa Dog 1972; Fire, Lightning, Explosion, Aircraft Damage.

THIRD REICH AND ROLL (Torso CD 405)
Hitler was a Vegetarian, Swastikas on Parade.
Bonus tracks. Satisfaction, Loser Weed, Beyond the Valley in a Day in the Life, Flying.

FINGERPRINCE (Torso CD 407)
You yesyesyes, Home Age Conversation, Godsong, March de la Winni, Bossy, Boo Who? Tourniquet of Roses Youyesyesyes Again, Six Things to a Cycle.
Bonus tracks Babyfingers EP; Death in Barstow, Melon Collie Lassie, Flight of the Bumble Roach, Walter Westinghouse.

DUCK STAB/BUSTER AND GLEN (Torso CD 406)

Constantinople, Sinister Exaggerator, The Booker Tease, Blue Rosebuds, Laughing Song, Bach is Dead, Elvis and His Boss, Lizard Lady, Semolina, Birthday Boy, Weight-Lifting Lulu, Krafty Cheese, Hello Skinny, The Electrocutioner.
Bonus Tracks: *Goosebump* from Diskomo; Disaster, Plants, Farmers, Twinkle.

NOT AVAILABLE (Torso CD 414)

Edweena, The Making of a Soul, Ship's A 'Going Down, Never Known Questions, Epilogue.
Bonus Tracks. Selections from Title in Limbo: Intro, The Shoe Salesman, Crashing, Monkey & Bunny, Mahogany Wood, The Sailor Song.

ESKIMO (Torso CD 404)

The Walrus Hunt, Birth, Artic Hysteria, The Angry Angakok, A Spirit Steals a Child, The Festival of Death
Bonus tracks. Resident tracks from Subterranean Modern compilation; I Left My Heart In San Francisco, Dumbo The Clown (Who Loved Christmas), Is He Really Bringing Roses, (The Replacement) Time's Up.

THE COMMERCIAL ALBUM (Torso CD 413)

Forty one minute wonders!
Bonus Tracks; More one minute wonders!

MARK OF THE MOLE (Torso CD 417)

VOICES OF THE AIR, THE ULTIMATE DISASTER - Won't you keep us Working?, First Warning, Back to Normality? The Sky Falls! Why are we Crying? The Tunnels are Filling, It Never Stops.
MIGRATION - March to the Sea, The Observer, Hole-Workers' New Hymn.
ANOTHER LAND - Rumours, Arrival, Deployment, Saturation.
THE NEW MACHINE - Idea, Construction, Failure/reconstruction, Success.
FINAL CONFRONTATION - Driving the Moles away, Don't Tread On Me, The Short War, Resolution?

Bonus Tracks : Intermission Music: Lights Out, Shorty's Lament. The Moles Are Coming, Would We Be Alive? The New Hymn.

THE TUNES OF TWO CITIES (Torso CD 418)

Serenade for Missy, A Maze of Jigsaws, Mousetrap, God of Darkness, Smack your Lips (Clap Your Teeth) Praise for the Curse, The Secret Seed, Smokebeams, Mourning the Undead, Song of the Wild, The Evil Disposer, Happy Home (Excerpt from Act II of Innisfree).
Bonus tracks: Anvil Forest, Scent of Mint. (Not on LP)

THE RESIDENTS MOLE SHOW; LIVE IN HOLLAND (Torso CD 420)

Voices of the Air, The Secret Seed, narration, The Ultimate Disaster, narration, God of Darknes, narration, Migration, narration, Smack Your Lips, narration, Another Land, narration, The New Machine, narration, Call of The Wild, Final Confrontation, narration, Satisfaction, Happy Home.

GEORGE AND JAMES (Korova Kode9 LP)

GEORGE - Rhapsody In Blue, I Got Rhythm, Summertime
JAMES -Live At The Apollo; I'll Go Crazy, Try Me, Think, I Don't Mind, Lost Someone, Please, Please, Please, Night Train.

THE BIG BUBBLE (Torso CD 419)

Sorry, Hop a Little, Go Where Ya Wanna Go, Gotta Gotta Get, Cry for the Fire, Die-Stay-Go, Vinegar, Firefly, The Big Bubble, Fear for the Future, Kula Bocca Says So.
Bonus Tracks: Safety is a Cootie Wootie; Pt. 1 Prelude for a Toddler, Pt. 2 Toddler Lullaby, Pt. 3 Safety is the Cootie Wootie.

WHATEVER HAPPENED TO VILENESS FATS/CENSUSTAKER (Torso CD 204)

Whatever Happened to Vileness Fats? Atomic Shopping Carts, Adventures of a Troubled Heart, Search for the Short Man, The Importance of Evergreen, Broccoli and Saxophone, Disguised as Meat, Thoughts Busily Betraying, Lord, It's Lonely, The Knife Fight.
Selected tracks from Census Taker.

13TH ANNIVERSARY SHOW: LIVE IN HOLLAND (Torso CD 018)

Jailhouse Rock, Where is She? Picnic in the Jungle, I Got Rhythm, Passing the Bottle, Monkey and Bunny, This is a Man's Man's Man's World, Walter Westinghouse, Easter Woman Guitar Solo, Diskomo, Hello Skinny, Constantinople, Hop a Little, Cry For the Fire, Kamakazi Lady (Encore).

STARS AND HANK FOREVER (Torso CD 022)

HANK: Hey Good Lookin', Six More Miles (to the Graveyard) Kaw-Liga, Ramblin' Man, Jambalaya.
SOUSASIDE: Nobles of the Mystic Shrine, The Stars and Stripes Forever, El Capitan, The Liberty Bell, Sempers Fidelis, The Washington Post.

GOD IN THREE PERSONS (Torso CD 055)

Main Titles (God in Three Persons), Hard and Tenderly, Devotion? The Thing About Them, Their Early Years, Loss of Loved One, The Touch, The Service, Confused (By What I felt Inside), Fine Fat Flies, Time, Silver, Sharp and Could Not Care, Kiss of Flesh, Pain and Pleasure.

THE KING AND EYE (Torso CD 137)

Blue Suede Shoes, the Baby King Part 1, Don't Be Cruel, Heartbreak Hotel, All Shook Up, Return to Sender, the Baby King Part 2, Teddy Bear, Devil in Disguise, Stuck on You, Big Hunk o' Love, A Fool Such As I, the Baby King part 3, Little Sister, His Latest Flame, Burning Love, Viva Las Vegas, the Baby King Part 4, Love Me Tender, the Baby King Part 5, Hound Dog.

CUBE E - LIVE IN HOLLAND (Torso CD 169)

BUCKEROO BLUES; From the Plains to Mexico, The Theme from Buckeroo Blues, The Stampede, The Trail Dance, Bury Me Not, Cowboy Waltz, Saddle Sores, The Theme from Buckeroo Blues (reprise).
BLACK BARRY: The Gospel Truth, Shortnin' Bread, Balck Berry, Fourty-Four, Engine 44, New Orleans, Voodoo Queen, What am I Gonna Do, Organism.

THE BABY KING: Ober, The Baby King 1, Don't Be Cruel, Evil In Disguise, Burning Love, Teddy Bear, Love Me Tender, The Baby King 2, Hound Dog/Out.

FREAK SHOW (Torso CD 183)

Everyone Comes to the Freak Show, Harry the Head, Herman the Human Mole, Wanda the Worm Woman, Jack the Boneless Boy, Benny the Bouncing Bump, Mickey the Mumbling Midget, Lillie, Nobody Laughs When They Leave

OUR FINEST FLOWERS (Euro Ralph CD001)

Gone Again, The Sour Song, Six Amber Things, Mr. Lonely, Perfect Goat, Blue Tongues, Jungle Bunny, I'm Dreaming of a White Sailor, Or Maybe a Marine, Kick a Picnic, Dead Wood, Baby Sister, Forty-Four No More, He Also Serves, Ship of Fools, Be Kind To U-WEB Footed Friends.

OTHER CDs

There were also a number of CD's issued through The Residents second Fan Club UWEB (1988-93).

SANTA DOG (UWEB 0001)

SNAKEY WAKE (UWEB 0002)

BUCKEROO BLUES (UWEB 0003)

LIVER MUSIC (UWEB 0004)

DAY DREAM B-LIVER (UWEB 0005)

13TH ANNIVERSARY LIVE IN USA (UWEB 0006)

STRANGER THAN SUPPER

(This was a comercially availiable compilation of some of the above material.)

As UWEB is no more, these CD's are no longer availiable although the newly formed Ralph America and Euro Ralph may possibly be selling them by mail order in the near future.

VIDEO

THE EYE SCREAM. - Contains most of Residents promo films as well as footage of live shows. Hosted by Penn and Teller. Homer Flynn and Hardy Fox (The Men from the Cryptic Corporation) also make an appearance.

THE MOLE SHOW/WHATEVER HAPPENED TO VILENESS FATS. Self explanatory.

OTHER MEDIA

Twenty Twisted Questions. Laserdisc. Similar to Eyes Scream
Freak Show CD-ROM.
FREAK SHOW comic (Dark Horse Comics Inc.)

OTHER RECOMMENDED RECORDINGS

The Residents sound is unique although musical elements and technique can be detected in some of the following recordings. Of course, they are recommended here in their own right.

SUN RA

Sun Ra issued over 115 LP's. Try the following recent reissues for size:
WE TRAVEL THE SPACEWAYS/BAD AND BEAUTIFUL (EVIDENCE ECD 22040-2) An absolute classic and a must for any early Residents fan.
JAZZ IN SILHOUETTE (EVIDENCE ECD 22012-2) (Recorded in 1958 the track Ancient Aiethopia sounds remarkably like a slowed down Land Of 1,000 dances.)
COSMIC TONES FOR MENTAL THERAPY/ART FORMS OF DIMENSIONS TOMMORROW (EVIDENCE ECD 22036). Innovative. Avant-Garde and experimenting with the effects of echo.

FAUST

Highly original studio based band. All recordings highly recommended especially...
FAUST (Japanese Polydor CD re-issue) Blinding experimental 1971 debut. First thirty seconds gives The Beatles and the Rolling Stones a sonic going over. The seed that spawned *Third Reich and Roll?* A classic.

HARRY PARTCH

Obviously. Hard to get hold of his stuff these days but check out two reissued CD's:

THE MUSIC OF HARRY PARTCH (CRI CD 7000)

THE BEWITCHED (CRI CD 7001)

Unfortunately, neither contain the six part suite entitled *Barstow*. If you like "Six Things To A Cycle" you'll love this stuff.

STAN KENTON

Kenton was a highly successful dance band leader in the 1940s and was not afraid to experiment with "progressive Jazz" and more orchestral forms although as his career progressed he returned to a more commercial footing. There are many Kenton CD's on the market. Most recommended:

KENTON IN HI-FI (CAPITOL CDP7984512)

This is where Kenton re-recorded some of his most popular tunes from the '40s including the million seller "Eager Beaver" and "Machito" which turn up on *The Tunes Of Two Cities* as "Mousetrap" and "Happy Home".

PEREZ PRADO

Cuban born Prado was the man who put the mambo on the map and drove Mexico and then America wild with it in the early '50s. The Residents loved his horn arrangements as well as his distinctive rhythms and borrowed freely. Sadly, they have yet to produce a cover of the famous "Mambo No 5". Highly Recommended:

GO GO MAMBO (Tumbaq TCD-013)

Prado's breakthrough Mexican recordings. Guaranteed to make your toes twitch and have you bellowing "Unh!" at the top of your voice.

VOODOO SUITE/EXOTIC SUITE (Bear Family Records BCD 15463)

Two LP's on one CD. Prado experiments with longer suite-like pieces. Also 'covers' a few jazz standards in his particular rhythmic style. Great music.

HENRY MANCINI

Highly under-rated film score composer. Best known for his "Pink Panther Theme" which has some great Pradoish/Kentonesque horns.

FRANK ZAPPA

An obvious influence. Zappa not only pioneered psychedelia but also revealed how a total command of studio technique could produce highly original work. His music is a melting pot of styles; rock, jazz, contemporary classical, depraved humour and satire. His output (like The Residents) is huge. Recommended:
WE'RE ONLY IN IT FOR THE MONEY/LUMPY GRAVY (Zappa Records CDZAP13)

CAPTAIN BEEFHEART

One of rock's lost treasures. Like The Residents, totally distinctive and totally original. Beefheart mixed lyrical poerty with unusual instrumentation and time signatures. Gave up music in 1982 to concentrate upon painting and by all accounts doing very well out of it. Recommended:
TROUT MASK REPLICA (Reprise 2027-2)
Seminal Zappa produced outing "The Blimp" is fantastic.
THE SPOTLIGHT KID/CLEAR SPOT (Reprise 7599 26249-2)
Double CD compilation of two classic LPs, particularly Clear Spot.

RALPH RECORDS

Ralph was founded by The Residents in 1972 to release their recordings. Home of the infamous "Buy or Die" catalogue, it is now exclusively Residents orientated and carries recordings, video, art, and collectibles.

Ralph America

109 Minna Street,
Suite 391, San Francisco, CA 94105,
USA
1-800-795-3933 (USA)
FAX 415/543-8982

Euro Ralph

Cremon 32
DW 2000 Hamburg 11,
Germany
FAX (49) 040-374550

T.E.C. Tones

T.E.C. Tones was founded by former Ralph manager, Tom Timony. T.E.C. Tones carries Residents products, as well as recordings by other independent artists. It is also known for buying and selling Residents collectibles.

T.E.C. Tones
PO Box 1477,
Hoboken, NJ 07030
USA.
201/420-0238
FAX 201/420-6494

The Residents are managed by:
The Cryptic Corporation
566 Folsom Street,
San Francisco, CA 94105
415/543-8248
FAX 415/543-8982

Other music titles available from SAF Publishing.

KRAFTWERK - Man, Machine And Music
by Pascal Bussy

200 pages – paperback – 8 page photo section – ISBN 0946719 098
Price £11.95

"The mechanical universe of Kraftwerk has been cloned or copied in Detroit, Brussels, Milan, Manchester, and even psychedelicised by the delerium of house music. You can define it as you want; sci-fi music, techno-disco, cybernetic rock. But the term I prefer even so is robot pop. It fits in with our objective which consists of working without respite toward the construction of the perfect pop song for the tribes of the global village." Ralf Hütter (Kraftwerk)

Rock writer Pascal Bussy has written a uniquely definitive account of Kraftwerk's history, delving beyond their publicity shunning exterior. Ralf Hütter, Florian Schneider, former group members and collaborators have broken their usual silence, providing an in-depth examination into their working methods and complex technological imagery.

"Bussy engagingly explains why they're one of the few groups who've actually changed how music sounds." **** Q Magazine

"Bussy's crisp, business-like biography purrs along like one of the top-of-the-range Mercs Ralf Hütter and Florian Schneider used to collect." NME

"I doubt that this book will ever be bettered." Vox

"What you get – as might be expected from Monsieur Bussy, author of the excellent The Can Book – is a wealth of analysis of the music and plenty of insights into the methods and motives behind the group, often from Ralf and Florian themselves." Top Magazine

CABARET VOLTAIRE - The Art of the Sixth Sense
by Mick Fish & Dave Hallbery

224 pages – paperback - Over 50 photographs - ISBN 0946719 039
Price: £6.95

Over their 20 year history Cabaret Voltaire have instinctively and mischieviously gnawed away at the accepted ideas about sound and visual presentation in pop music, evolving from their earliest Dadaist dabblings through to being vigorous exponents of a radical new dance music.

Now into its second and updated edition, this definitive book is a critical appraisal of the career of an innovative and influential group.

"Instead of straight-forward chronological narrative, Messers Hallbery and Fish have opted for a more illuminating interview approach and the chapters cover everything from video and voodoo to Dada and Doublevision, with a separate section on ex-member Chris Watson, plenty of pics and a lengthy discography. An essential and lively read." Sounds

"A fabulous book which really lifts itself above the mire that is the tacky pop music book world. Essential reading." Zipcode Magazine

"What little can be gleaned about the two characters through their music – and despite umpteen albums that wouldn't be much - here they tell all." Sheffield Star

"This is an alternative music book in the true sense. An excellent read, not just for the hardcore fan!" Impulse Magazine

WIRE... Everybody Loves A History
by Kevin Eden

192 pages – paperback – Over 70 photographs - ISBN 0946719 071
Price: £9.95.

Wire were one of the most intriguing and unpredictable bands to have
arisen out of the punk era. Including interviews and commentary
about Wire's complete history and solo projects, Kevin Eden
successfully unravels the complexities of this multi-faceted group.

*"Eden delivers a sharp portrayal of the punk industry's behaviour,
influence and morality."* **** Q Magazine

"Any band or their fans could feel well served by a book like Eden's."
Vox Magazine

*"Everybody Loves A History is a fine complement to the band's music,
from its self-effacing title to the sheer wealth of interview and
photographic material."* Record Collector

*"This is an enlightening and enjoyable read with decent pics (a rare
thing in biogs)."* Time Out

"An amazing book". Music From The Empty Quarter

The CAN Book
by Pascal Bussy & Andy Hall

192 pages - paperback - Over 80 photographs - ISBN 0946719 055
Price: £8.95

From The Buzzcocks to The Fall, The Jesus and Mary Chain through
to Verve, Can's joyously anarchic music continues to influence a host
of contemporary musicians. Pascal Bussy has compiled a complete
history of this 'cult' band, including biographies of individual members,
a full chronology and discography.

*"If Can's music is a mystery, this book will make you want to
investigate."* Q Magazine

*"A book trying to make sense of their myths and weird psyches has
never been more welcome."* Sounds

*"Bussy's account of the characters and chronology of Can is helpfully
musicalogical for the fan and iced generously enough with information
and anecdotes to attract the as-yet unaligned."* Melody Maker

TAPE DELAY
by Charles Neal

256 pages - paperback - Over 60 photographs - ISBN 0946719 020
Price £11.95

Recently reprinted, Tape Delay is a unique collection of interviews and exclusive writing which is now widely recognised as a definitive document of the underground groups of the '80s.

Features: Marc Almond, Cabaret Voltaire, Nick Cave, Chris & Cosey, Coil, Einstürzende Neubauten, The Fall, Foetus, Diamanda Galas, The Hafler Trio, Matt Johnson, Laibach, Lydia Lunch, New Order, Psychic TV, Boyd Rice, Henry Rollins, Sonic Youth, Swans, Test Dept and many more.

"A virtual Who's Who of people who've done the most in the past decade to drag music out of commercial confinement."
"Tape Delay investigates those rare underground performers who've stuck their forefingers up the butt of commercial (in)sensibility to pursue their own visions. On that level alone it should be welcomed." NME

By far the most ambitious attempt so far to link together the large number of noise-orientated bands to have emerged from the indie ghetto." Sounds

"Overall, this is a truly superb book which anyone even half interested in any of the artists covered should invest in." Impulse Magazine

"Arguably the best genre book of all time." Music From The Empty Quarter.

"Useful and timely." i-D Magazine

"Intriguing and interesting" Q Magazine

Forthcoming Title:

Wrong Movements - A Robert Wyatt History
by Mike King

160 pages - A4 format - ISBN 0946719 101 - Publication date Spring 1994.

Robert Wyatt was a founding member of The Soft Machine, who along with Pink Floyd helped to transform the late '60s psychedelic scene in England into something more lasting. Through successive Lps, Soft Machine moved toward a more jazz-based fusion with rock music, punctuated by Wyatt's distinctive drumming and vocals.

After helping to compose much of Soft Machine's most compelling material, Wyatt left to pursue a solo career, ultimately forming Matching Mole, producing two critically acclaimed LP's only to disband prematurely.

In 1973, Wyatt fell from a third floor window during a drunken incident at a party. The accident left him paralysed from the waist downwards. Undeterred he threw his efforts into solo recordings which were now based around his increasing grasp of simple and effective keyboard melody lines, accompanied by lyrics filled with poignant personal and political references. The results were both haunting and reflective, even producing two chart hits – his 1974 re-working of "I'm a Believer", and the 1983 Falklands War indictment "Shipbuilding" written especially for him by Elvis Costello.

Mike King's meticulous biography pieces together a chronological account of Wyatt's 30 year career. *Wrong Movements* is punctuated by interview material from Robert Wyatt himself, as well as Kevin Ayers, Hugh Hopper, Daevid Allen, Andy Summers, Keith Tippett, Carla Bley, Fred Frith and many, many more. These contributions are mixed with press clippings and details about Robert's music, concerts and recordings to produce a fascinating document about one of rock music's most neglected figures.

Ordering/Mail Order:

All titles are available from most good bookshops, or order from your local bookshop quoting the ISBN number, author, title and publisher.

To order direct by mail order contact:
Wings Mail Order, Freepost, London, N7 8BR, UK
Telephone: 071 704 7063 Fax: 071 607 6714
Payment can be made by cheque or Access/Visa/Eurocard

Distribution:

UK & Europe: Airlift Book Co, 26-28 Eden Grove, London. N7 8EF
Tel: 071-607 5792 Fax: 071-607 6714

USA: Inland Book Company, PO Box 120261, East Haven, Connecticut 06512, USA. Tel: 203 467 4257 Fax: 203 467 8364.
Or:
See Hear, 59 East 7th Street, New York, NY10003, USA.
Tel: 212 982 6968 Fax: 212 387 8017

Canada: Marginal Distribution, Unit 103, 277 George Street North, Peterborough, Ontario, Canada K9J 3G9. Tel: 705 745 2326

Titles also available through Virgin Records, Tower Records (USA), Rough Trade Shop, Compendium Bookshop, These Records, Sordide Sentimentale (France), Touch.

SAF Publishing Ltd. 12 Conway Gardens, Wembley, Middx. HA9 8TR.
England. Telephone: 081 – 904 6263